101 Crochet Stitches

with International Crochet Symbols
and Terms in English, French,
Spanish, German and Italian

Bobbie Matela, Managing Editor
Carol Wilson Mansfield, Art Director
Mary Ann Frits, Editorial Director
Kelly Robinson and Sandy Scoville, Pattern Editors
Ann Campbell, Illustrations
Graphic Solutions inc-chgo, Book Design

Patterns tested and models made by Lori Llewellyn and Hannelore Southard.

We have made every effort to ensure the accuracy and completeness of these instructions. We cannot, however, be responsible for human error, typographical mistakes, or variations in individual work.

©1995 by American School of Needlework®, Inc.; ASN Publishing, 1455 Linda Vista Drive, San Marcos, CA 92069

ISBN: 0-88195-693-7   All rights reserved.   Printed in U.S.A.   1 2 3 4 5 6 7 8 9

About This Book

This book is a wonderful reference of 101 Pattern Stitches for crochet. You will be able to use these patterns with any crochet thread or yarn you choose to create everything from doilies to afghans.

In addition to our usual American-style English instructions, we have shown each Pattern Stitch in international symbols. The symbols we used and the stitches they represent are shown on pages 4-7. Also included are the words used for each stitch in the United States, the United Kingdom, and by French, Spanish, German and Italian speaking crocheters.

Contenu

Ce manuel de référence comporte 101 points de crochet que l'on peut réaliser avec tous les types de fils à crocheter. Inspirez-vous en pour vos créations, du napperon à la couverture.

Outre les instructions usuelles en anglais, vous trouverez des symboles internationaux pour chaque point. Les symboles utilisés et les points auxquels ils font référence sont repris aux pages 4-7. Vous trouverez également la liste des termes utilisés pour les différents points aux Etats-Unis et au Royaume-Uni, ainsi que par les amateurs de crochet, de langue francaise, espagnole, allemande et italienno.

Sobre Esta Libro

Este libro es una referencia excelente de 101 diseños para la labor de ganchillo. Ud, puede utilizar estos diseños con el tipo de hilo de su selección, para creaciones tan variadas como tapetes o mantas de lana hechas de ganchillo.

Además de nuestras instrucciones en inglés, al estilo norteamericano, también presentamos todos los diseños con simbolos internacionales. Los simbolos usados y los puntos correspondientes han sido indicados en las páginas 4-7. También han sido incluidas -para cada punto- las palabras usadas en los EE.UU. ei R.U., y por los aficionados del punto de ganchillo en Francia, España, Alemania e Italia.

Zu diesem Buch

Dies Buch ist ein herrliches Referenzwerk - 101 musterstiche für häkelarbeiten. Diese Muster können mit jedem Häkelgarn Ihrer Wahl eingesetzt werden, um alles zu erstellen, von kleinen Zierdeckchen bis hin zu afghanischen Teppichen.

Neben den englischsprachigen Anweisungen im amerikanischen Stil zeigen wir außerdem jeden Musterstich in internationalen Symbolen. Die benutzten Symbole und deren Bedeutung werden auf den Seiten 4-7 erklärt. Außerden finden Sie die Worte, welche für jeden Stich in den USA und England benutzt werden, sowie diese Begriffe auf Deutsch, Französisch, Spanisch und Italienisch, für Häkler aus diesen Ländern.

Di Questo Libro

Questo libro é una referenza utilissima per 101 lavori all'uncinetto. Potrete usare questi campioni con qualunque filo o filato da lavoro all'uncinetto che sceglierete per creare tutto, da centrini a coperte.

In aggiunta a nostre istruzioni inglesi usate in America, abbiamo rappresentato ogni campione di punto in simboli internazionali. I simboli che abbiamo usato e i punti che rappresentano sono mostrati alle pagine 4-7. Sono anche inclusi i termini usati per ogni punto in inglese (Stati Uniti e Regno Unito) e in francese, spagnolo, tedesco e italiano.

Stitch Review

Symbol	Name		Stitch
◯	**U.S.**	chain	
	U.K.	chain	
	Francais	maille en l'air (ml)	
	Español	cadeneta (cad)	
	Deutsch	Luftmasche (Lftn)	
	Italienno	punto catenella	
+	**U.S.**	single crochet (sc)	
	U.K.	double crochet (dc)	
	Francais	maille serrée	
	Español	punto bajo (pb)	
	Deutsch	Feste Masche (fM)	
	Italienno	maglia bassa (m. bassa)	
⊤	**U.S.**	double crochet (dc)	
	U.K.	treble (tr)	
	Francais	bride (br)	
	Español	punto alto doble (pad)	
	Deutsch	Stäbchen (Stb)	
	Italienno	maglia alta (m. alta)	
T	**U.S.**	half double crochet (hdc)	
	U.K.	half treble (htr)	
	Francais	demi-bride (demi-br)	
	Español	punto alto (pa)	
	Deutsch	Halbe Stäbchen (h.Stb)	
	Italienno	mezza maglia alta	
⊤	**U.S.**	triple crochet (trc)	
	U.K.	double treble (dtr)	
	Francais	double bride (d-br)	
	Español	punto alto triple (pat)	
	Deutsch	Doppel-stäbchen (D-Stb)	
	Italienno	maglia altissima	
●	**U.S.**	slip stitch (sl st)	
	U.K.	slip stitch (sl st)	
	Francais	maille coulee	
	Español	punto enano (pe)	
	Deutsch	Kettmasche	
	Italienno	maglia bassissima	

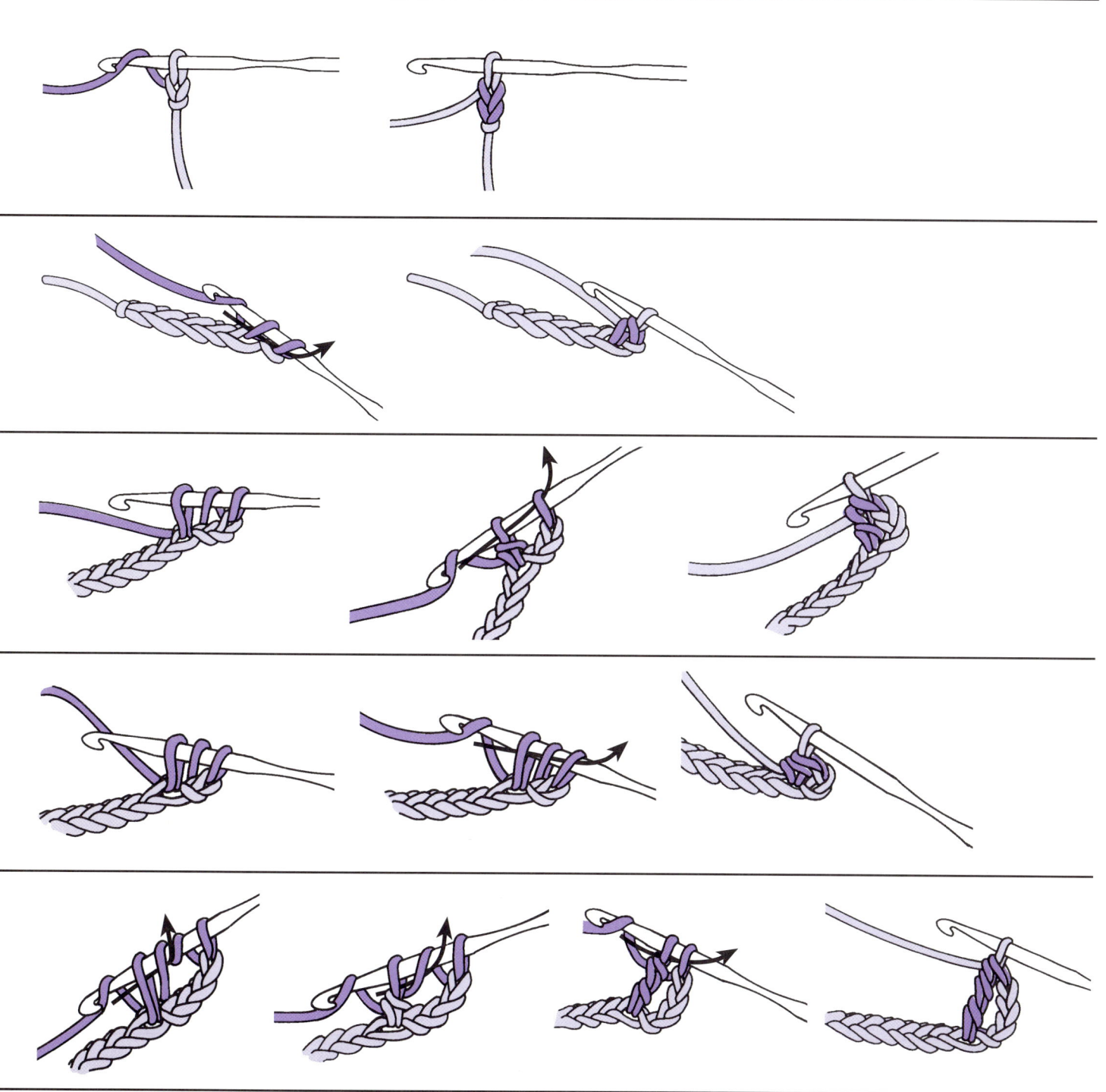

Stitch Review

Symbol	Name		Stitch
	U.S.	picot	
	U.K.	picot	
	Francais	picot (pi)	
	Español	piquito	
	Deutsch	Pikot (Pi)	
	Italienno	pippiolino	
	U.S.	cluster (CL)	
	U.K.	cluster (CL)	
	Francais	grappe	
	Español	puntos altos cerrados en el mismo punto	
	Deutsch	Büschelmasche	
	Italienno	maglia raggruppata	
	U.S.	popcorn (PC)	
	U.K.	popcorn (PC)	
	Francais	popcorn	
	Español	puntos altos cerrados juntas con una cadeneta	
	Deutsch	popcorn-Masche	
	Italienno	nocciolina	
	U.S.	front post (FP)	
	U.K.	front post (FP)	
	Francais	double bride en relief avant	
	Español	punto alto triple en relieve por delante de la labor	
	Deutsch	vorderes Maschenglied	
	Italienno	in costa davanti	
	U.S.	back post (BP)	
	U.K.	back post (BP)	
	Francais	double bride en relief arrière	
	Español	punto alto triple en relieve por detras de la labor	
	Deutsch	hinteres Maschenglied	
	Italienno	in costa dietro	

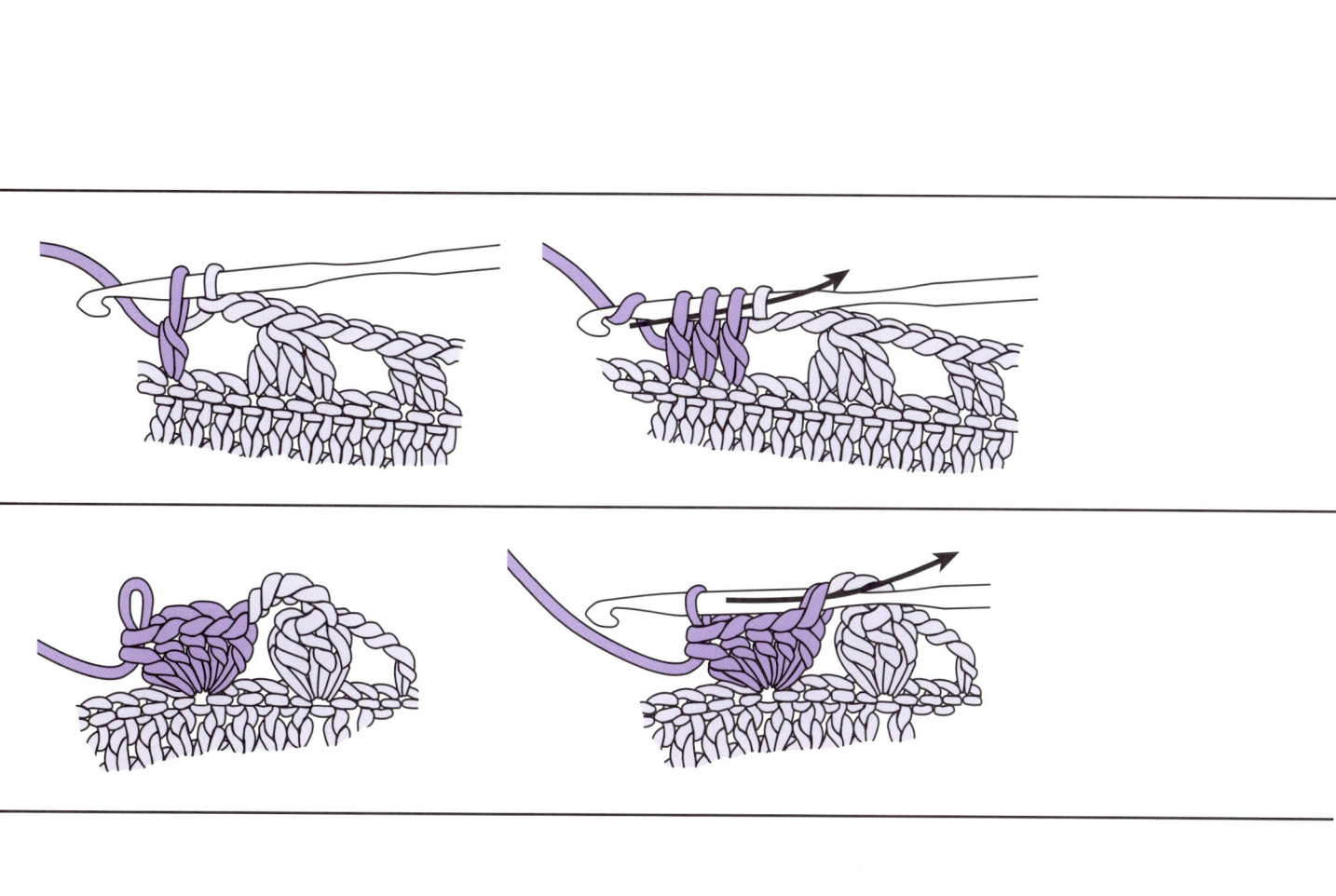

Abbreviations and Symbols (for written instructions)

beg	begin(ning)
bl(s)	back loop(s)
BPdc	back post double crochet(s)
ch(s)	chain(s)
CL(s)	cluster(s)
dc	double crochet(s)
dtrc	double triple crochet(s)
fl(s)	front loop(s)
FPdc	front post double crochet(s)
hdc	half double crochet(s)
lp(s)	loop(s)
patt	pattern
prev	previous
rem	remain(ing)
rep	repeat(ing)
rnd(s)	round(s)
sc	single crochet(s)
sk	skip
sl	slip
sl st(s)	slip stitch(es)
sp(s)	space(s)
st(s)	stitch(es)
tog	together
trc	triple crochet(s)
YO	yarn over

* An asterisk is used to mark the beginning of a portion of instructions to be worked more than once; thus, "rep from * twice more" means after working the instructions once, repeat the instructions following the asterisk twice more (3 times in all).

† The dagger identifies a portion of instructions that will be repeated again later in the same row or round.

: The number after a colon at the end of a row or round indicates the number of stitches you should have when the row or round has been completed.

( ) Parentheses are used to enclose instructions which should be worked the exact number of times specified immediately following the parentheses, such as "(2 sc in next dc, sc in next dc) twice." They are also used to set off and clarify a group of stitches that are to be worked all into the same space or stitch, such as "(2 dc, ch 1, 2 dc) in corner sp."

[ ] Brackets and ( ) parentheses are used to provide additional information to clarify instructions.

Join - join with a sl st unless otherwise specified.

Front loop is the loop toward you at the top of the stitch.

Back loop is the loop away from you at the top to the stitch.

Post is the vertical part of the stitch.

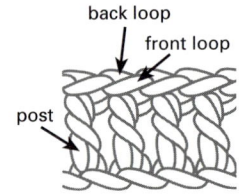

Metric Conversion Charts

CROCHET HOOKS CONVERSION CHART

U.S.	1	2	3	4	5	6	7	8	9	10	11	12	13	14
English	3/0	2/0	1/0	1	1½	2	2½	3	4	5	5½	6	6½	7
Continental-mm	3	2.5		2		1.75	1.5	1.25	1	0.75		0.6		

CROCHET HOOKS CONVERSION CHART

U.S.	1/B	2/C	3/D	4/E	5/F	6/G	8/H	9/I	10/J	10½/K
English	12	11	10	9	8	7	6	5	4	2
Continental-mm	2.25	2.75	3.25	3.5	3.75	4.25	5	5.5	6	6.5

Reading The Charts

The chart for each pattern shows it from the **right side**.

The first row of a pattern is sometimes the right side of the work, and sometimes the wrong side. When the first row is the right side, follow the chart from right to left for the first row; when the first row is the wrong side, follow the chart from left to right for the first row. The arrow on each chart shows where to begin Row 1.

Numbers appearing on the right-hand side of each chart correspond to row numbers as given in the written instructions.

Multiples

A multiple is the number of chains required for each repeat of the stitch pattern; to this we may then add a specified number of chains to make the pattern end correctly.

If a pattern specifies a multiple of 6 + 2, for example, you need to make a starting chain in multiples of 6 (12, 18, 24, etc); and then add a final 2 chains. The number of chains given after the + sign in a multiple is added only once.

Helpful Hint: When working a long foundation chain, add a few extra chains to ensure that the first row of the pattern will not run out of chains; then at the end of the first row, rip out any extra chains.

Before You Begin

Unlike most crochet patterns, those in this book specify no gauge, no material requirements, and no hook sizes.

That's because each stitch can be worked in your choice of yarn or thread to vary the size and appearance of each stitch to fit your project.

The photos below show the same stitch pattern worked in four different weights of materials and four different hook sizes, giving four different looks.

When choosing the material and hook for your project, you may wish to do some experimenting with a variety of materials until you achieve the appearance and texture that pleases you.

The stitch patterns photographed on the following pages were all made with sport weight yarn and a size F aluminum hook.

Bedspread weight thread

Baby weight yarn

Sport weight yarn

Worsted weight yarn

#1

Multiple of 12 + 8

Row 1: Sc in 2nd ch from hook; * ch 3, sk next 2 chs, sc in next ch; rep from * across; ch 4, turn.

Row 2 (right side): Sc in next ch-3 lp, ch 3; * sc in next ch-3 lp, 3 dc in next sc; (sc in next ch-3 lp, ch 3) 3 times; rep from * across to last ch-3 lp; sc in last ch-3 lp, 2 dc in last sc; ch 3, turn.

Row 3: Dc in first dc, 2 dc in next dc; * (sc in next ch-3 lp, ch 3) twice; sc in next ch-3 lp, 2 dc in each of next 3 dc; rep from * across to last ch-3 lp; sc in last ch-3 lp, ch 3, sc in 3rd ch of turning ch-4; ch 4, turn.

Row 4: * Sc in next ch-3 lp, 2 dc in each of next 6 dc; sc in next ch-3 lp, ch 3; rep from * across to last 3 dc; 2 dc in each of last 3 dc; ch 1, turn.

Row 5: Sc in next dc, ch 3, sk next 2 dc, sc between last dc skipped and next dc; * ch 3, sc in next ch-3 lp, (ch 3, sk next 3 dc, sc between last dc skipped and next dc) 3 times; rep from * across to turning ch; ch 3, sc in 3rd ch of turning ch-4; ch 3, turn.

Row 6: Dc in first sc; * (sc in next ch-3 lp, ch 3) 3 times; sc in next ch-3 lp, 3 dc in next sc; rep from * across to last sc; ch 1, dc in last sc; ch 1, turn.

Row 7: Sc in next dc, ch 3; * sc in next ch-3 lp, 2 dc in each of next 3 dc; (sc in next ch-3 lp, ch 3) twice; rep from * across to turning ch; dc in 3rd ch of turning ch-3; ch 3, turn.

Row 8: Dc in first dc, 2 dc in each of next 2 dc; * sc in next ch-3 lp, ch 3, sc in next ch-3 lp, 2 dc in each of next 6 dc; rep from * across to last sc; ch 1, dc in last sc; ch 1, turn.

Row 9: Sc in next dc; * ch 3, sk next 3 dc, sc between last dc skipped and next dc, (ch 3, sk next 3 dc, sc between last dc skipped and next dc) twice; ch 3, sc in next ch-3 lp; rep from * across to turning ch; ch 3, sc in 3rd ch of turning ch-3; ch 4, turn.

Rep Rows 2 through 9 for pattern.

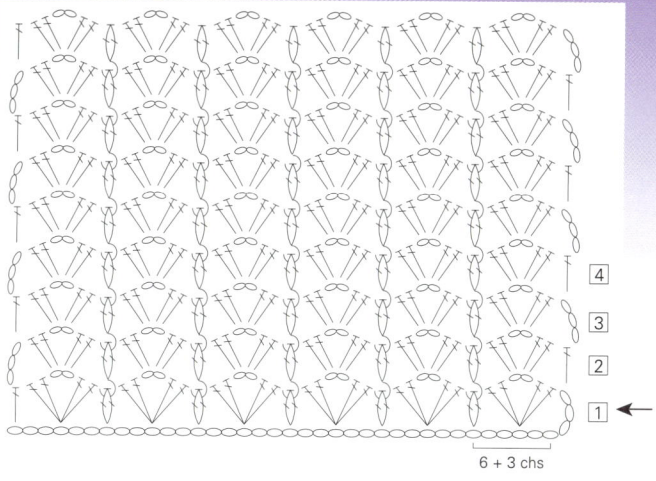

6 + 3 chs

#2

Multiple of 6 + 3

PATTERN STITCH

Cluster (CL): Keeping last lp of each dc on hook, 2 dc in next st, YO and draw through all 3 lps on hook: CL made.

Front Post Cluster (FPCL): Keeping last lp of each dc on hook and inserting hook from front to back to front, 2 dc around post (see page 8) of next st, YO and draw through all 3 lps on hook: FPCL made.

Back Post Cluster (BPCL): Keeping last lp of each dc on hook and inserting hook from back to front to back, 2 dc around post (see page 8) of next st, YO and draw through all 3 lps on hook: BPCL made.

Row 1 (right side): In 6th ch from hook work (2 dc, ch 2, 2 dc); * sk next 2 chs, CL (see Pattern Stitches) in next ch; sk next 2 chs, in next ch work (2 dc, ch 2, 2 dc); rep from * across to last 3 chs; sk next 2 chs, dc in last ch; ch 3, turn.

Row 2: * In next ch-2 sp work (2 dc, ch 2, 2 dc); BPCL (see Pattern Stitches) around next CL; rep from * across to last ch-2 sp; in last ch-2 sp work (2 dc, ch 2, 2 dc); sk next 2 dc, dc in 5th ch of beg 5 skipped chs; ch 3, turn.

Row 3: * In next ch-2 sp work (2 dc, ch 2, 2 dc); FPCL (see Pattern Stitches) around next BPCL; rep from * across to last ch-2 sp; in last ch-2 sp work (2 dc, ch 2, 2 dc); sk next 2 dc, dc in 3rd ch of turning ch-3; ch 3, turn.

Row 4: * In next ch-2 sp work (2 dc, ch 2, 2 dc); FPCL around next CL; rep from * across to last ch-2 sp; in last ch-2 sp work (2 dc, ch 2, 2 dc); sk next 2 dc, dc in 3rd ch of turning ch-3; ch 3, turn.

Rep Rows 3 and 4 for pattern.

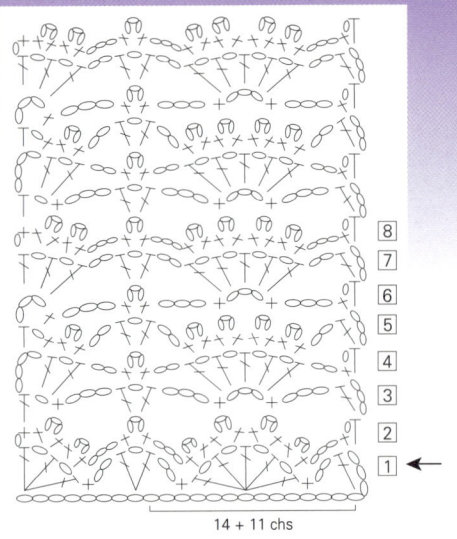

14 + 11 chs

#3

Multiple of 14 + 11

Row 1 (right side): Dc in 4th ch from hook, ch 2, sk next 2 chs, sc in next ch, sk next 3 chs; * in next ch work (dc, ch 1) 4 times; dc in same ch; sk next 3 chs, sc in next ch, ch 2, sk next 2 chs, in next ch work (dc, ch 1, dc); ch 2, sk next 2 chs, sc in next ch, sk next 3 chs; rep from * across to last ch; in last ch work (dc, ch 1, dc, ch 1, dc); ch 1, turn.

Row 2: Sc in next dc, in each of next 2 ch-1 sps work (sc, ch 3, sc); ch 3; * in next ch-1 sp work (sc, ch 3, sc); ch 3, in each of next 4 ch-1 sps work (sc, ch 3, sc); ch 3; rep from * across to last dc; sk last dc, in 3rd ch of beg 3 skipped chs work (sc, ch 1, hdc); ch 3, turn.

Row 3: Dc in first hdc, ch 3; * sk next 2 ch-3 lps, sc in next ch-3 lp, ch 3, sc in next ch-3 lp, ch 3, sk next 2 ch-3 lps, in next ch-3 lp work (dc, ch 1, dc); ch 3; rep from * across to last 3 ch-3 lps; sk next 2 ch-3 lps, sc in last ch-3 lp, ch 1, sk next sc, dc in last sc; ch 4, turn.

Row 4: In next ch-1 sp work (dc, ch 1, dc); * ch 2, in next ch-1 sp work (sc, ch 3, sc); ch 2, sk next ch-3 lp, in next ch-3 lp work (dc, ch 1) 4 times; dc in same lp; rep from * across to turning ch; ch 2, in 3rd ch of turning ch-3 work (sc, ch 1, hdc); ch 3, turn.

Row 5: Dc in first hdc; * ch 2, sk next ch-2 sp, in each of next 4 ch-1 sps work (sc, ch 3, sc); ch 2, sk next ch-2 sp, in next ch-3 lp work (dc, ch 1, dc); rep from * across to last ch-1 sp; ch 2, in last ch-1 sp work (sc, ch 3, sc); sc in turning ch lp, ch 1, hdc in 3rd ch of turning ch-4; ch 3, turn.

Row 6: Sc in next ch-1 sp; * ch 3, sk next ch-3 lp and next ch-2 sp, in next ch-1 sp work (sc, ch 3, sc); ch 3, sk next ch-2 sp and next ch-3 lp, sc in next ch-3 lp, ch 3, sc in next ch-3 lp; rep from * across to turning ch; in 3rd ch of turning ch-3 work (sc, ch 1, hdc); ch 3, turn.

Row 7: Dc in first hdc; * ch 2, sk next ch-3 lp, in next ch-3 lp work (dc, ch 1) 4 times; dc in same lp; ch 2, sk next ch-3 lp, in next ch-3 lp work (dc, ch 1, dc); rep from * across to turning ch; ch 2, in turning ch lp work (dc, ch 1, dc, ch 1, dc); ch 1, turn.

Row 8: Sc in next dc, in each of next 2 ch-1 sps work (sc, ch 3, sc); ch 3; * in next ch-1 sp work (sc, ch 3, sc); ch 3, in each of next 4 ch-1 sps work (sc, ch 3, sc); ch 3; rep from * across to last dc; sk last dc, in 3rd ch of turning ch-3 work (sc, ch 1, hdc); ch 3, turn.

Rep Rows 3 through 8 for pattern.

20 + 18 chs

#4

Multiple of 20 + 18

PATTERN STITCH

Cluster (CL): Keeping last lp of each dc on hook, 2 dc in st, YO and draw through all 3 lps on hook: CL made.

Row 1 (right side): Sc in 2nd ch from hook; * ch 5, sk next 3 chs, sc in next ch; rep from * across; ch 6 (counts as first trc and ch-2 sp on following rows), turn.

Row 2: Sc in next ch-5 lp, ch 5, sc in next ch-5 lp, in next sc work [CL (see Pattern Stitch), ch 3, CL]; * sc in next ch-5 lp; (ch 5, sc in next ch-5 lp) 4 times; in next sc work (CL, ch 3, CL); rep from * across to last ch-5 lp; sc in last ch-5 lp, ch 2, trc in last sc; ch 1, turn.

Row 3: Sc in next trc, ch 5, sc in next ch-5 lp; * in next sc work (CL, ch 3, CL); sc in next ch-3 lp, in next sc work (CL, ch 3, CL); sc in next ch-5 lp, (ch 5, sc in next ch-5 lp) 3 times; rep from * across to turning ch; ch 5, sc in 4th ch of turning ch-6; ch 6, turn.

Row 4: Sc in next ch-5 lp, ch 5, sc in next ch-3 lp; * in next sc work (CL, ch 3, CL); sc in next ch-3 lp, (ch 5, sc in next ch-5 lp) 4 times; rep from * across to last 2 ch-5 lps; sc in next ch-5 lp, ch 5, sc in last ch-5 lp, ch 2, trc in last sc; ch 1, turn.

Row 5: Sc in next trc; * ch 5, sc in next ch-5 lp, ch 5, sc in next ch-3 lp, (ch 5, sc in next ch-5 lp) twice; in next sc work (CL, ch 3, CL); sc in next ch-5 lp; rep from * across to turning ch; ch 5, sc in 4th ch of turning ch-6; ch 6, turn.

Row 6: * Sc in next ch-5 lp, (ch 5, sc in next ch-5 lp) 3 times; in next sc work (CL, ch 3, CL); sc in next ch-3 lp, in next sc work (CL, ch 3, CL); rep from * across to last sc; ch 2, trc in last sc; ch 1, turn.

Row 7: Sc in next trc; * (ch 5, sc in next ch-5 lp) 3 times; ch 5, sc in next ch-3 lp, in next sc work (CL, ch 3, CL); sc in next ch-3 lp; rep from * across to turning ch; ch 5, sc in 4th ch of turning ch-6; ch 6, turn.

Row 8: Sc in next ch-5 lp, ch 5, sc in next ch-5 lp; * in next sc work (CL, ch 3, CL); (sc in next ch-5 lp, ch 5) twice; sc in next ch-3 lp, (ch 5, sc in next ch-5 lp) twice; rep from * across to last sc; ch 2, trc in last sc; ch 1, turn.

Rep Rows 3 through 8 for pattern.

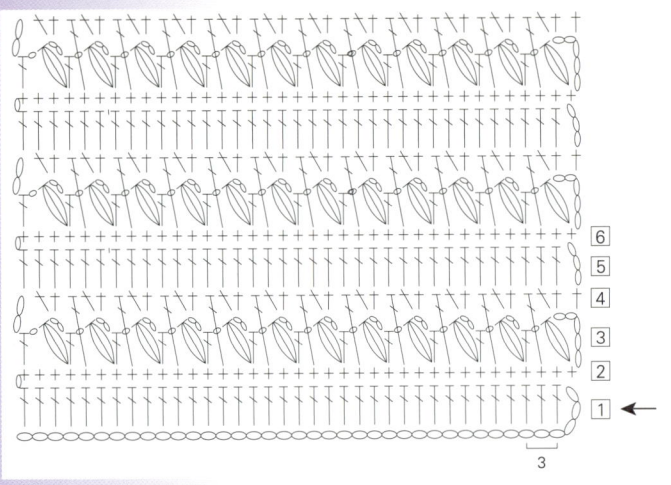

3

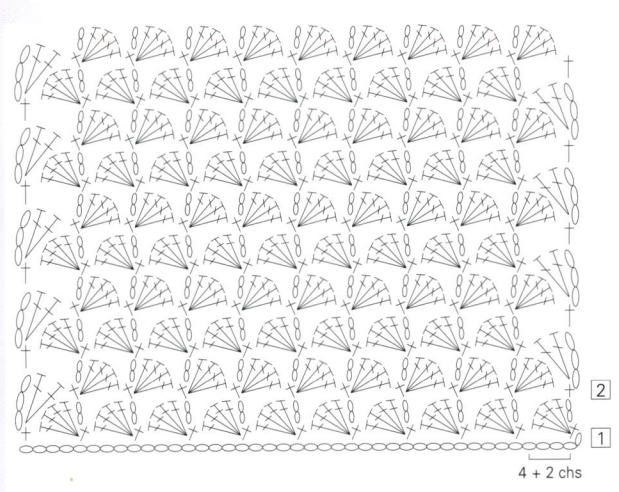

4 + 2 chs

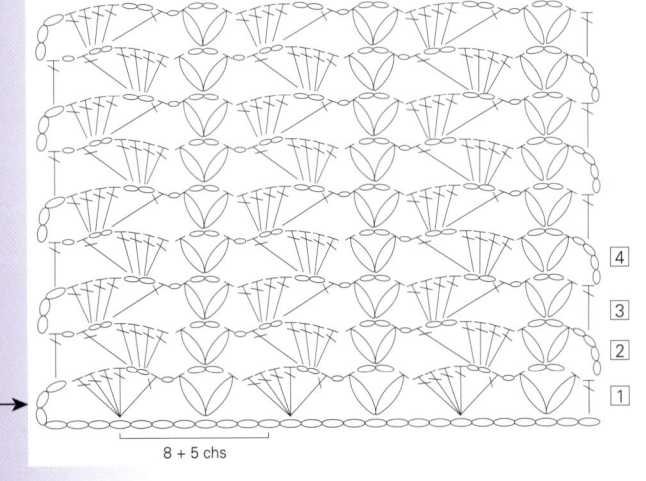

8 + 5 chs

#5

Multiple of 3

> **PATTERN STITCH**
>
> **Cluster** (CL): YO, draw up lp in next st, (YO, draw up lp in same st) twice; YO and draw through all 7 lps on hook: CL made.

Row 1 (right side): Dc in 4th ch from hook and in each rem ch; ch 1, turn.

Row 2: Sc in each dc to beg 3 skipped chs; sc in 3rd ch of 3 skipped chs; ch 5, turn.

Row 3: CL (see Pattern Stitch) in first sc; ch 1, sk next 2 sc; * in next sc work (dc, ch 2, CL); ch 1, sk next 2 sc; rep from * across to last sc; dc in last sc; ch 2, turn.

Row 4: 2 sc in next ch-2 sp; * working over next ch-1 sp, working behind prev row, dc in next sc on 2nd row below, 2 sc in next ch-2 sp; rep from * across to turning ch lp; 2 sc in lp; sc in 3rd ch of turning ch-5; ch 3, turn.

Row 5: Dc in each st to turning ch; dc in 2nd ch of turning ch-2; ch 1, turn.

Row 6: Sc in each dc across to turning ch; sc in 3rd ch of turning ch-5; ch 5, turn.

Rep Rows 3 through 6 for pattern.

#6

Multiple of 4 + 2

Row 1: Sc in 2nd ch from hook; * ch 2, 4 dc in same ch; sk next 3 chs, sc in next ch; rep from * across; ch 3, turn.

Row 2: 2 dc in first sc; sk next 4 dc, sc in next ch; * ch 2, 4 dc over side of last sc made; sk next 4 dc, sc in next ch; rep from * across; ch 3, turn.

Rep Row 2 for pattern.

#7

Multiple of 8 + 5

> **PATTERN STITCH**
>
> **Cluster** (CL): (YO, insert hook in st, YO and draw lp through) twice; YO and draw through all 5 lps on hook: CL made.

Row 1: In 7th ch from hook work (4 dc, ch 2, dc); * ch 1, sk next 3 chs, in next ch work [CL (see Pattern Stitch), ch 2, CL]; sk next 3 chs, in next ch work (4 dc, ch 2, dc); rep from * across to last 2 chs; sk next ch, dc in last ch; ch 4, turn.

Row 2 (right side): * In next ch-2 sp work (CL, ch 2, CL); in next ch-2 sp work (4 dc, ch 2, dc); ch 1; rep from * across to last ch-2 sp; in last ch-2 sp work (4 dc, ch 2, dc); ch 1, dc in 3rd ch of beg 6 skipped chs; ch 3, turn.

Row 3: In next ch-2 sp work (4 dc, ch 2, dc); * ch 1, in next ch-2 sp work (CL, ch 2, CL); in next ch-2 sp work (4 dc, ch 2, dc); rep from * across to turning ch; dc in 3rd ch of turning ch-4; ch 4, turn.

Row 4: * In next ch-2 sp work (CL, ch 2, CL); in next ch-2 sp work (4 dc, ch 2, dc); ch 1; rep from * across to turning ch; dc in 3rd ch of turning ch-3; ch 3, turn.

Rep Rows 3 and 4 for pattern.

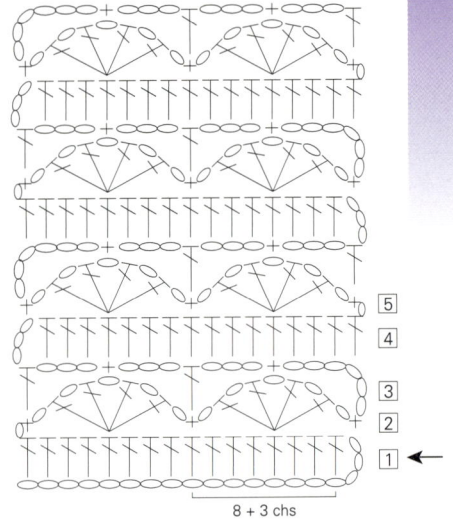

#8

Multiple of 8 + 3

Row 1 (right side): Dc in 4th ch from hook (3 skipped chs count as a dc) and in each rem ch; ch 1, turn.

Row 2: Sc in next dc; * ch 1, sk next 3 dc, in next dc work (dc, ch 1) 4 times; sk next 3 dc, sc in next dc; rep from * across to beg 3 skipped chs; sc in 3rd ch of 3 skipped chs; ch 6 (counts as first dc and ch-3 lp on following rows), turn.

Row 3: * Sk next 2 ch-1 sps, sc in next ch-1 sp, ch 3, dc in next sc, ch 3; rep from * across to last sc; dc in last sc; ch 3 (counts as first dc on following rows), turn.

Row 4: * Dc in next 3 chs, in next sc, in next 3 chs, and in next dc; rep from * across to turning ch; dc in next 4 chs of turning ch-6; ch 1, turn.

Row 5: Sc in next dc; * ch 1, sk next 3 dc, in next dc work (dc, ch 1) 4 times; sk next 3 dc, sc in next dc; rep from * across to turning ch; sc in 3rd ch of turning ch-3; ch 6, turn.

Rep Rows 3 through 5 for pattern.

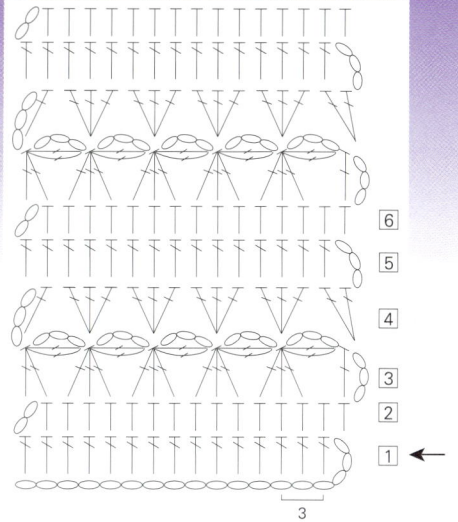

Multiple of 3

PATTERN STITCHES

Cluster (CL): Keeping last lp of each dc on hook, 2 dc in st, YO and draw through all 3 lps on hook: CL made.

3-dc Cluster (3-dc CL): Keeping last lp of each dc on hook, dc in next 3 sts, YO and draw through all 4 lps on hook: 3-dc CL made.

Row 1 (right side): Dc in 4th ch from hook and in each rem ch; ch 2 (counts as first hdc on following rows), turn.

Row 2: Hdc in each dc to beg 3 skipped chs; hdc in 3rd ch of 3 skipped chs; ch 3 (counts as first dc on following rows), turn.

Row 3: Dc in first hdc, ch 3, CL (see Pattern Stitches) in top of dc just made, sk next hdc; * 3-dc CL (see Pattern Stitches) over next 3 hdc; ch 3, CL in top of 3-dc CL just made; rep from * across to last hdc; dec over last hdc and turning ch (to work dec: YO, draw up lp in next hdc, YO, draw through 2 lps on hook; YO, draw up lp in 2nd ch of turning ch-2, YO, draw through 2 lps on hook; YO and draw through all 3 lps on hook: dec made); ch 3, turn.

Row 4: Dc in first dc; * 3 dc in top of next 3-dc CL; rep from * across to turning ch; 2 dc in 3rd ch of turning ch-3; ch 3, turn.

Row 5: Dc in each dc to turning ch; dc in 3rd ch of turning ch-3; ch 2, turn.

Row 6: Hdc in each dc to turning ch; hdc in 3rd ch of turning ch-3; ch 3, turn.

Rep Rows 3 through 6 for pattern.

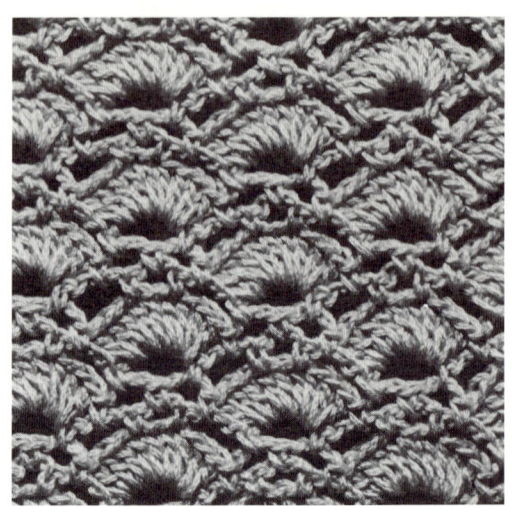
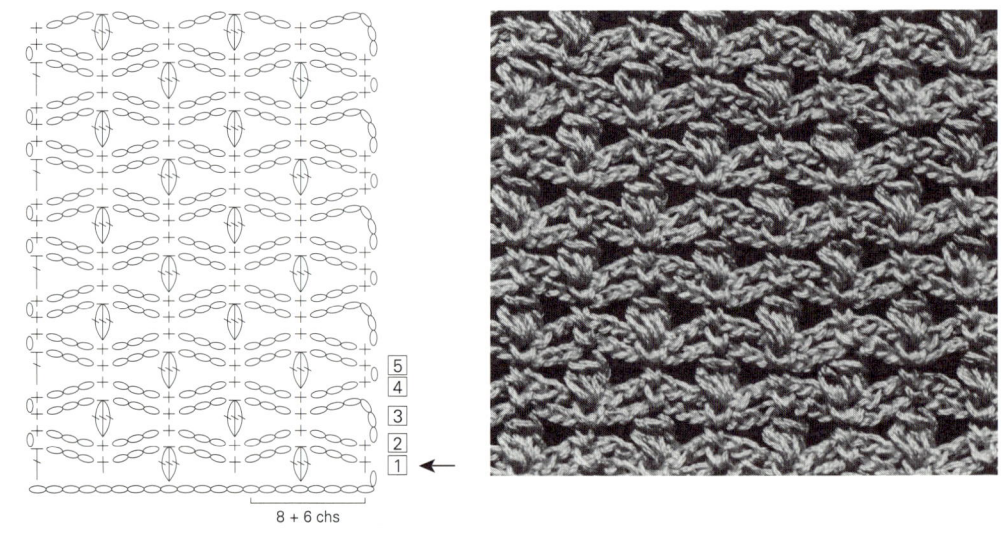
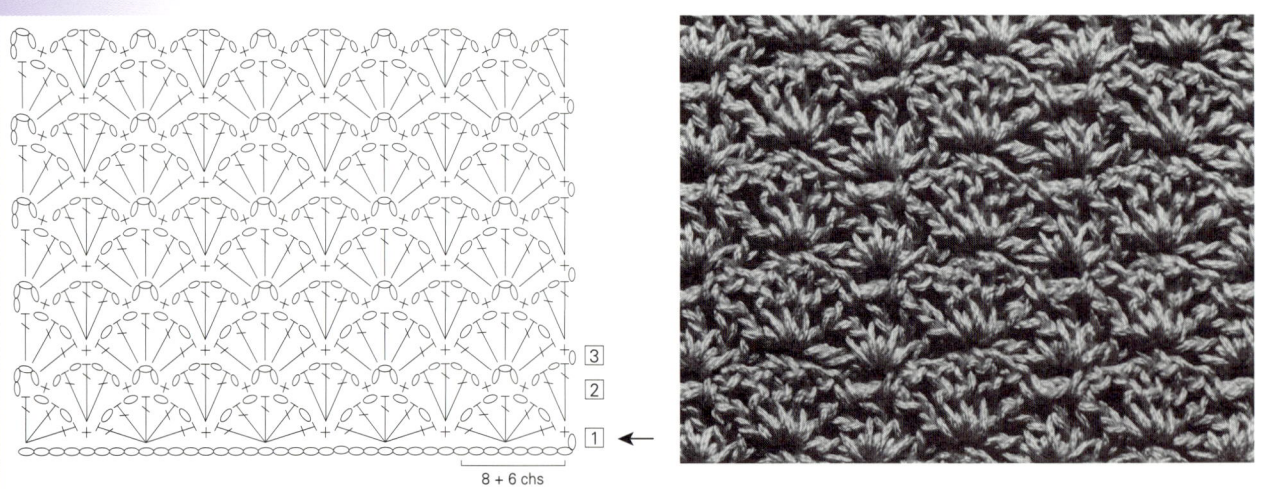

#10

Multiple of 15 + 14

Row 1: Sc in 6th ch from hook; * ch 5, sk next 5 chs, sc in next ch, (ch 3, sk next 2 chs, sc in next ch) 3 times; rep from * across to last 8 chs; ch 5, sk next 5 chs, sc in next ch, ch 1, sk next ch, hdc in last ch; ch 1, turn.

Row 2 (right side): Sc in next hdc; * 9 dc in next ch-5 lp; (sc in next ch-3 lp, ch 3) twice; sc in next ch-3 lp; rep from * across to beg 5 skipped chs; sc in 4th ch of 5 skipped chs; ch 6, turn.

Row 3: * Sk next 3 dc, sc in next dc, ch 3, sk next dc, sc in next dc, ch 3, sc in next ch-3 lp, ch 5, sc in next ch-3 lp, ch 3; rep from * across to last sc; dc in last sc; ch 4, turn.

Row 4: * (Sc in next ch-3 lp, ch 3) twice; sc in next ch-3 lp, 9 dc in next ch-5 lp; rep from * across to turning ch lp; sc in lp, ch 1, dc in 3rd ch of turning ch-6; ch 5, turn.

Row 5: * Sc in next ch-3 lp, ch 5, sc in next ch-3 lp, ch 3, sk next 3 dc, sc in next dc, ch 3, sk next dc, sc in next dc, ch 3; rep from * across to turning ch; ch 2, dc in 3rd ch of turning ch-4; ch 1, turn.

Row 6: Sc in next dc; * 9 dc in next ch-5 lp; (sc in next ch-3 lp, ch 3) twice; sc in next ch-3 lp; rep from * across to turning ch; sc in 3rd ch of turning ch-5; ch 6, turn.

Rep Rows 3 through 6 for pattern.

#11

Multiple of 8 + 6

PATTERN STITCH

Cluster (CL): Keeping last lp of each dc on hook, 3 dc in next st, YO and draw through all 4 lps on hook: CL made.

Row 1 (right side): Sc in 2nd ch from hook; * ch 3, sk next 3 chs, CL (see Pattern Stitch) in next ch; ch 3, sk next 3 chs, sc in next ch; rep from * across to last 4 chs; ch 3, sk next 3 chs, dc in last ch; ch 1, turn.

Row 2: Sc in next dc, ch 3, sc in next sc; * ch 3, sc in next CL, ch 3, sc in next sc; rep from * across; ch 6, turn.

Row 3: Sk next sc, sc in next sc; * ch 3, CL in next sc; ch 3, sc in next sc; rep from * across; ch 1, turn.

Row 4: Sc in next sc, ch 3; * sc in next CL, ch 3, sc in next sc, ch 3; rep from * across to turning ch; sc in 3rd ch of turning ch-6; ch 1, turn.

Row 5: Sc in next sc; * ch 3, CL in next sc; ch 3, sc in next sc; rep from * across to last sc; ch 3, dc in last sc; ch 1, turn.

Rep Rows 2 through 5 for pattern.

#12

Multiple of 8 + 6

Row 1 (right side): Sc in 2nd ch from hook; * sk next 3 chs, in next ch work (dc, ch 1) 4 times; dc in same ch; sk next 3 chs, sc in next ch; rep from * across to last 4 chs; sk next 3 chs, in last ch work (dc, ch 1, dc, ch 1, dc); ch 4, turn.

Row 2: Sc in next ch-1 sp; * ch 1, in next sc work (dc, ch 1) 3 times; sk next ch-1 sp, sc in next ch-1 sp, ch 3, sc in next ch-1 sp; rep from * across to last sc; ch 1, in last sc work (dc, ch 1, dc); ch 1, turn.

Row 3: Sc in next dc; * in next ch-3 lp work (dc, ch 1) 4 times; dc in same lp; sk next dc, sc in next dc; rep from * across to turning ch lp; in lp work (dc, ch 1, dc, ch 1, dc); ch 4, turn.

Rep Rows 2 and 3 for pattern.

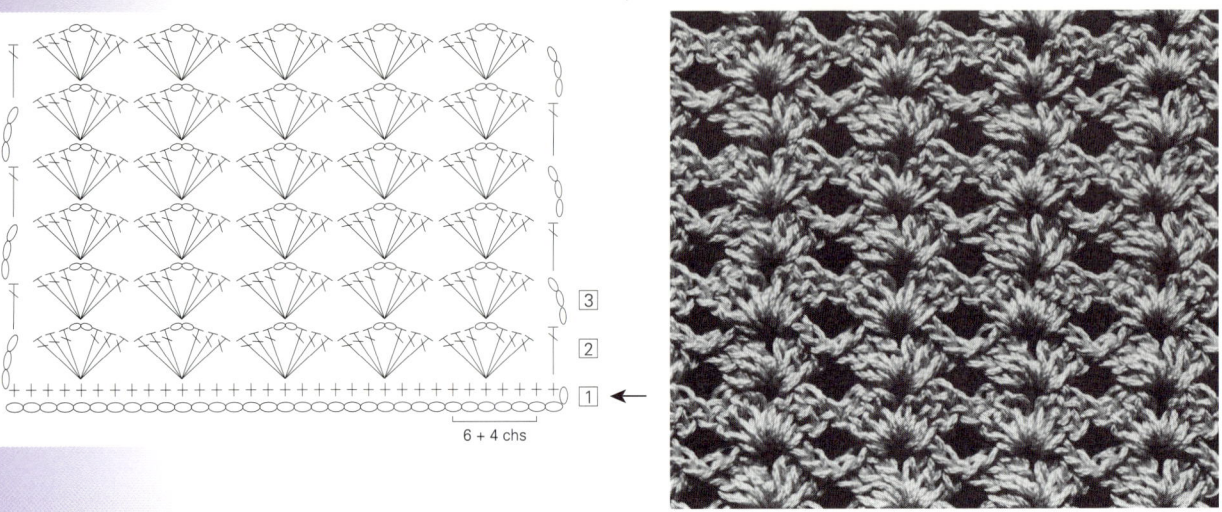

6 + 4 chs

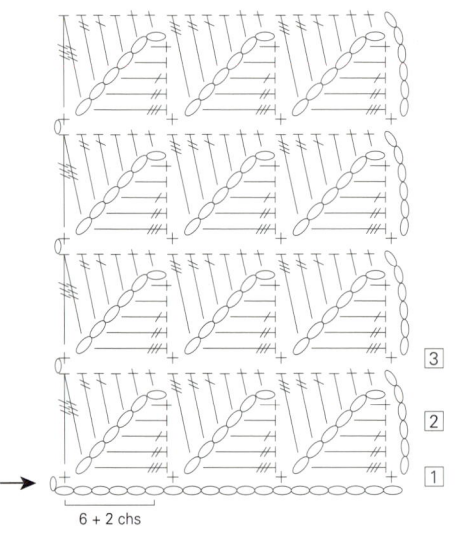

6 + 2 chs

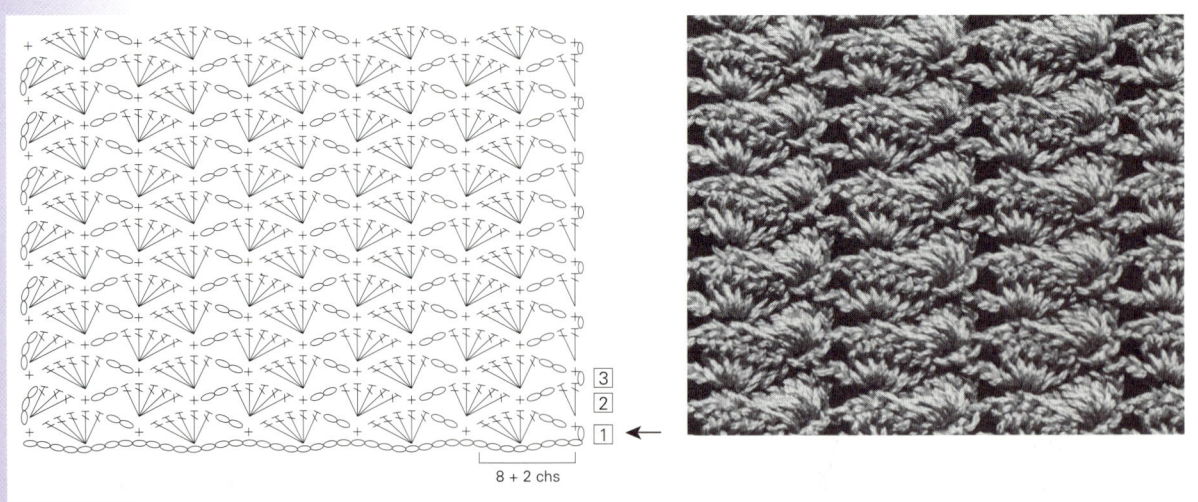

8 + 2 chs

#13

Multiple of 6 + 4

Row 1 (right side): Sc in 2nd ch from hook and in each rem ch; ch 3, turn.

Row 2: Sk next 4 sc, in next sc work (3 dc, ch 2, 3 dc): shell made; * sk next 5 sc, in next sc work (3 dc, ch 2, 3 dc): shell made; rep from * across to last sc; dc in last sc; ch 3, turn.

Row 3: Shell in ch-2 sp of each shell across to turning ch; dc in 3rd ch of turning ch-3; ch 3, turn.

Rep Row 3 for pattern.

#14

Multiple of 6 + 2

> **PATTERN STITCHES**
>
> **Double Triple Crochet** (dtrc): YO 3 times; draw up lp in next st, (YO and draw through 2 lps on hook) 4 times: dtrc made.
>
> **Cluster** (CL): Keeping last lp of each dtrc on hook, dtrc in next lp and in next sc, YO and draw through all 3 lps on hook: dtrc CL made.

Row 1: Sc in 2nd ch from hook; * ch 6, sc in 2nd ch from hook, hdc in next ch, dc in next ch, trc in next ch, dtrc (see Pattern Stitches) in next ch, sk next 5 chs, sc in next ch; rep from * across; ch 6, turn.

Row 2 (right side): * Working in unused lps of next 6 chs of prev row, sc in next 2 lps, hdc in next lp, dc in next lp, trc in next lp, dtrc in next lp; rep from * across to last unused lp of last ch-6; CL (see Pattern Stitches) over last unused lp and last sc; ch 1, turn.

Row 3: Sc in next CL; * ch 6, sc in 2nd ch from hook, hdc in next ch, dc in next ch, trc in next ch, dtrc in next ch, sc in next dtrc (on prev row); rep from * across to turning ch; sc in 6th ch of turning ch-6; ch 6, turn.

Rep Rows 2 and 3 for pattern.

#15

Multiple of 8 + 2

Row 1 (right side): Sc in 2nd ch from hook; * ch 2, sk next 3 chs, 5 dc in next ch; sk next 3 chs, sc in next ch; rep from * across; ch 3, turn.

Row 2: 3 dc in first sc; * sk next 3 dc, sc in next dc, ch 2, 5 dc in next sc; rep from * across to last sc; 2 dc in last sc; ch 1, turn.

Row 3: Sc in next dc; * ch 2, 5 dc in next sc; sk next 3 dc, sc in next dc; rep from * across to turning ch; sc in 3rd ch of turning ch-3; ch 3, turn.

Rep Rows 2 and 3 for pattern.

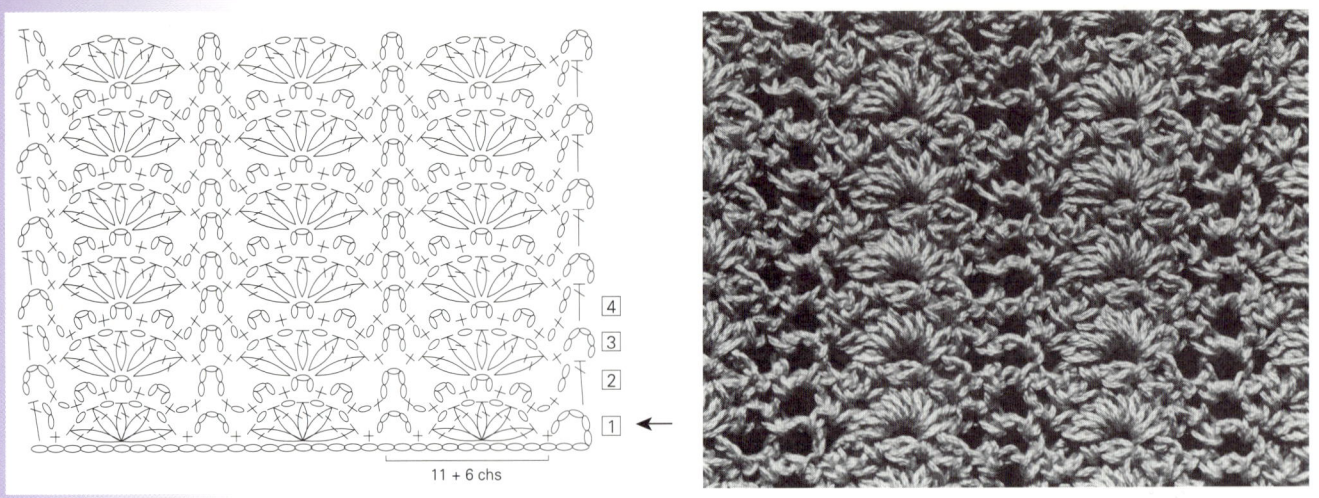

11 + 6 chs

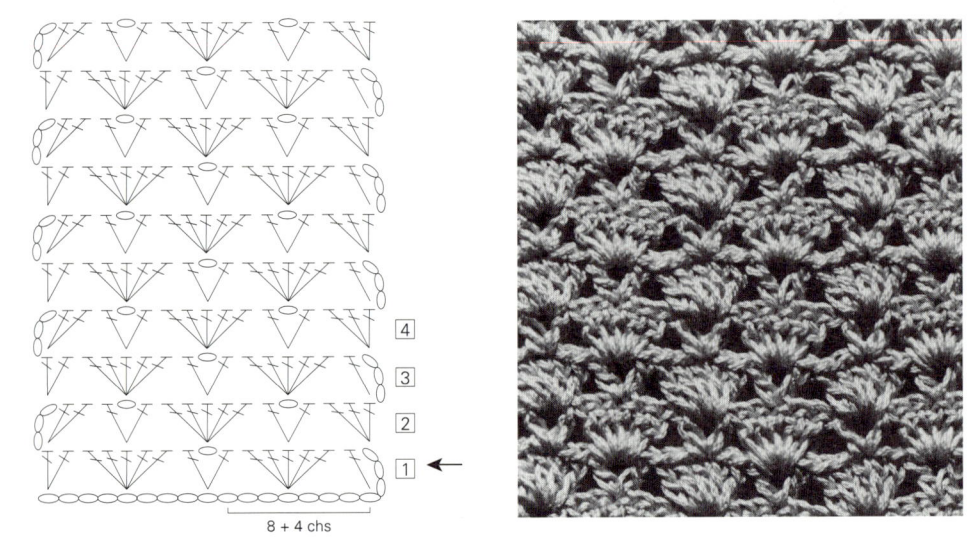

8 + 4 chs

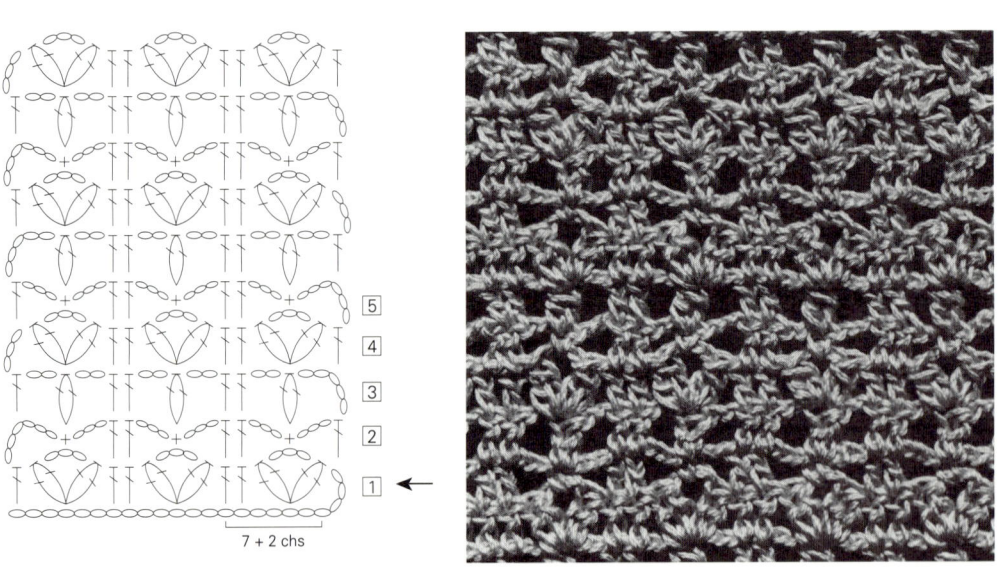

7 + 2 chs

#16

Multiple of 11 + 6

> **PATTERN STITCH**
>
> **Cluster** (CL): Keeping last lp of each dc on hook, 2 dc in next st, YO and draw through all 3 lps on hook: CL made.

Row 1 (right side): Sc in 8th ch from hook; * sk next 3 chs, in next ch work [CL (see Pattern Stitch), ch 1) 4 times; CL in same ch; sk next 3 chs, sc in next ch, ch 5, sk next 2 chs, sc in next ch; rep from * across to last ch; ch 2, dc in last ch; ch 5, turn.

Row 2: Sc in next ch-2 sp; * ch 1, (sc in next ch-1 sp, ch 3) 3 times; sc in next ch-1 sp, ch 1, in next ch-5 lp work (sc, ch 5, sc); rep from * across to lp formed by beg 7 skipped chs; ch 1, sc in lp, ch 2, dc in 5th ch of 7 skipped chs; ch 5, turn.

Row 3: Sc in next ch-2 sp; * sk next ch-3 lp, in next ch-3 lp work (CL, ch 1) 4 times; CL in same lp; in next ch-5 lp work (sc, ch 5, sc); rep from * across to turning ch lp; sc in lp, ch 2, dc in 3rd ch of turning ch-5; ch 5, turn.

Row 4: Sc in next ch-2 sp; * ch 1, (sc in next ch-1 sp, ch 3) 3 times; sc in next ch-1 sp, ch 1, in next ch-5 lp work (sc, ch 5, sc); rep from * across to turning ch lp; ch 1, sc in lp, ch 2, dc in 3rd ch of turning ch-5; ch 5, turn.

Rep Rows 3 and 4 for pattern.

#17

Multiple of 8 + 4

Row 1 (right side): Dc in 4th ch from hook; * sk next 3 chs, 5 dc in next ch; sk next 3 chs, in next ch work (dc, ch 1, dc); rep from * across to last ch; 2 dc in last ch; ch 3, turn.

Row 2: 2 dc in first dc; * sk next 3 dc, in next dc work (dc, ch 1, dc); 5 dc in next ch-1 sp; rep from * across to beg 3 skipped chs; 3 dc in 3rd ch of 3 skipped chs; ch 3, turn.

Row 3: Dc in first dc; * 5 dc in next ch-1 sp; sk next 3 dc, in next dc work (dc, ch 1, dc); rep from * across to turning ch; 2 dc in 3rd ch of turning ch-3; ch 3, turn.

Row 4: 2 dc in first dc; * sk next 3 dc, in next dc work (dc, ch 1, dc); 5 dc in next ch-1 sp; rep from * across to turning ch; 3 dc in 3rd ch of turning ch-3; ch 3, turn.

Rep Rows 3 and 4 for pattern.

#18

Multiple of 7 + 2

> **PATTERN STITCH**
>
> **Cluster** (CL): Keeping last lp of each dc on hook, 2 dc in next st, YO and draw through all 3 lps on hook: CL made.

Row 1 (right side): In 6th ch from hook work [CL (see Pattern Stitch), ch 3, CL]; * sk next 2 chs, dc in next 2 chs, sk next 2 chs, in next ch work (CL, ch 3, CL); rep from * across to last 3 chs; sk next 2 chs, dc in last ch; ch 6, turn.

Row 2: * Sc in next ch-3 lp, ch 3, dc in next 2 dc, ch 3; rep from * across to last ch-3 lp; sc in last ch-3 lp, ch 3, dc in 5th ch of beg 5 skipped chs; ch 5, turn.

Row 3: * CL in next sc; ch 2, dc in next 2 dc, ch 2; rep from * across to last sc; CL in last sc; ch 2, dc in 3rd ch of turning ch-6; ch 3, turn.

Row 4: * In next CL work (CL, ch 3, CL); dc in next 2 dc; rep from * across to turning ch; dc in 3rd ch of turning ch-5; ch 6, turn.

Row 5: * Sc in next ch-3 lp, ch 3, dc in next 2 dc, ch 3; rep from * across to last ch-3 lp; sc in last ch-3 lp, ch 3, dc in 3rd ch of turning ch-3; ch 5, turn.

Rep Rows 3 through 5 for pattern.

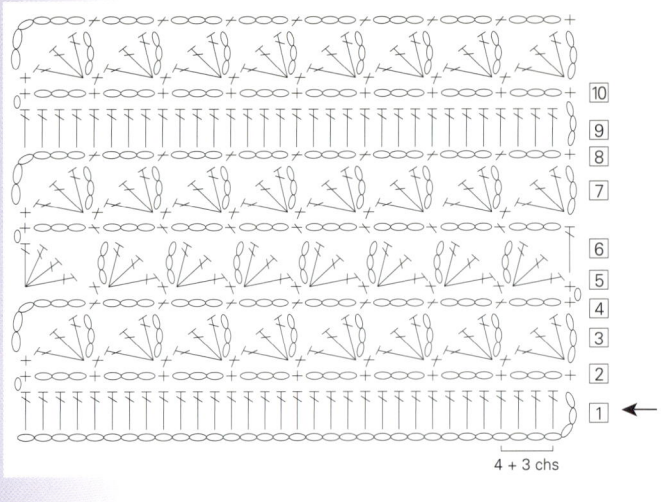

4 + 3 chs

12 + 2 chs

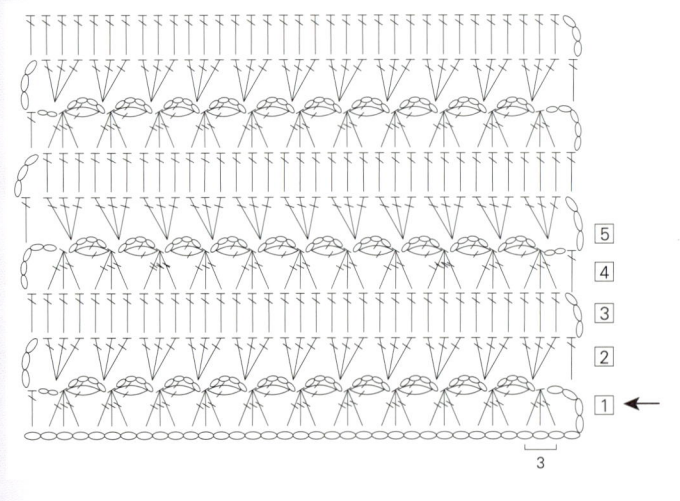

3

#19

Multiple of 4 + 3

Row 1 (right side): Dc in 4th ch from hook and in each rem ch; ch 1, turn.

Row 2: Sc in next dc; * ch 3, sk next 3 dc, sc in next dc; rep from * across to beg 3 skipped chs; sc in 3rd ch of 3 skipped chs; ch 3, turn.

Row 3: 3 dc in first sc; * in next sc work (sc, ch 3, 3 dc); rep from * across to last sc; sc in last sc; ch 6, turn.

Row 4: Sk next 3 dc, sc in next ch; * ch 3, sk next 3 dc, sc in next ch; rep from * across; ch 1, turn.

Row 5: Sc in next sc; * in next sc work (3 dc, ch 3, sc); rep from * across to turning ch; 4 dc in 3rd ch of turning ch-6; ch 1, turn.

Row 6: Sc in next dc; * ch 3, sc in 3rd ch of next ch-3 lp; rep from * across to last sc; ch 3, dc in last sc; ch 3, turn.

Row 7: Rep Row 3.

Row 8: Sk next 3 dc, sc in next ch; * ch 3, sk next 3 dc, sc in next ch; rep from * across; ch 3, turn.

Row 9: Dc in each ch and in each sc across to turning ch; dc in next 4 chs of turning ch-6; ch 1, turn.

Row 10: Sc in next dc; * ch 3, sk next 3 dc, sc in next dc; rep from * across to turning ch; sc in 3rd ch of turning ch-3; ch 3, turn.

Rep Rows 3 through 10 for pattern.

#20

Multiple of 12 + 2

Row 1: Sc in 2nd ch from hook; * ch 4, sk next 3 chs, sc in next ch; rep from * across; ch 4, turn.

Row 2 (right side): * Sc in next ch-4 lp, in next ch-4 lp work (3 dc, ch 3, 3 dc); sc in next ch-4 lp, ch 4; rep from * across to last ch-4 lp; sc in last ch-4 lp, ch 1, dc in last sc; ch 1, turn.

Row 3: Sc in next dc; * ch 4, in next ch-3 lp work (sc, ch 4, sc); ch 4, sc in next ch-4 lp; rep from * across to turning ch; ch 4, sc in 3rd ch of turning ch-4; ch 4, turn.

Rep Rows 2 and 3 for pattern.

#21

Multiple of 3

> **PATTERN STITCH**
>
> **Cluster** (CL): Keeping last lp of each dc on hook, dc in next 3 sts, YO and draw through all 4 lps on hook: CL made.
>
> **2-dc Cluster** (2-dc CL): Keeping last lp of each dc on hook, 2 dc in st, YO and draw through all 3 lps on hook: 2-dc CL made.

Row 1 (right side): CL (see Pattern Stitches) over 6th, 7th and 8th chs from hook; * ch 4, 2-dc CL (see Pattern Stitches) in 4th ch from hook; CL over next 3 chs; rep from * across to last 4 chs; CL over next 3 chs; ch 2, dc in last ch; ch 3 (counts as first dc on following rows), turn.

Row 2: Sk next ch, 3 dc in next ch; * sk next CL and next 3 chs, 3 dc in next ch; rep from * across to last CL; sk last CL, dc in 4th ch of beg 5 skipped chs; ch 3, turn.

Row 3: Dc in each dc across to turning ch; dc in 3rd ch of turning ch-3; ch 5 (counts as a dc and a ch-2 sp on following rows), turn.

Row 4: * CL over next 3 dc; ch 4, 2-dc CL in 4th ch from hook; rep from * across to last 3 dc; CL over next 3 dc; ch 2, dc in 3rd ch of turning ch-3; ch 3, turn.

Row 5: Sk next ch, 3 dc in next ch; * sk next CL and next 3 chs, 3 dc in next ch; rep from * across to last CL; sk last CL, dc in 3rd ch of turning ch-5; ch 3, turn.

Rep Rows 3 through 5 for pattern.

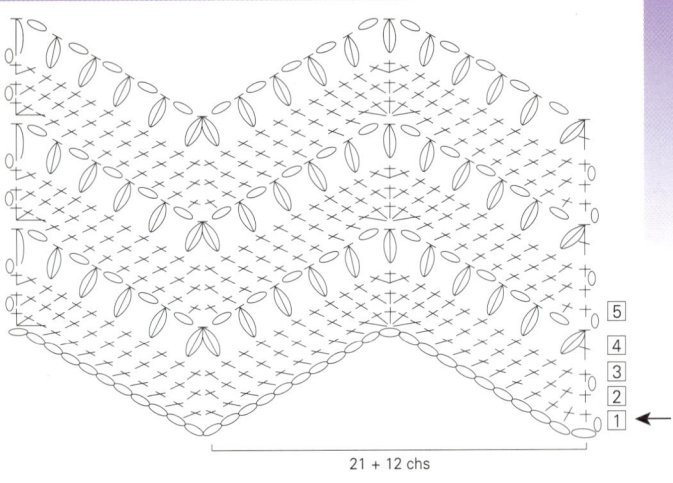

21 + 12 chs

#22

Multiple of 21 + 12

PATTERN STITCHES

Cluster (CL): YO, draw up lp in next st, (YO, and draw up in same st) twice; YO and draw through all 7 lps on hook: CL made.

Cluster decrease (CL dec): YO, draw up lp in next st, (YO, and draw up in same st) twice; sk next 2 sts, YO, draw up lp in next st, (YO, and draw up in same st) twice; YO and draw through all 13 lps on hook: CL dec made.

Row 1 (right side): Sc in 2nd ch from hook and in next 9 chs; * 5 sc in next ch; sc in next 9 chs, sk next 2 chs, sc in next 9 chs; rep from * across to last ch; 3 sc in last ch; ch 1, turn.

Row 2: 2 sc in next sc; sc in next 10 sc; * sk next 2 sc, sc in next 10 sc, 3 sc in next sc; sc in next 10 sc; rep from * across to last 2 sc; sk next sc, sc in last sc; ch 1, turn.

Row 3: Sc in next sc, sk next sc, sc in next 10 sc; * 3 sc in next sc; sc in next 10 sc, sk next 2 sc, sc in next 10 sc; rep from * across to last sc; 2 sc in last sc; ch 1, turn.

Row 4: YO, draw up lp in next sc, YO, draw up lp in same sc, YO and draw through all 5 lps; † ch 1, sk next sc, CL (see Pattern Stitches) in next sc †; rep from † to † 3 times more; * ch 1, sk next sc, CL dec (see Pattern Stitches) over next 4 sc; rep from † to † 9 times; rep from * across to last 4 sc; ch 1, sk next sc, YO, draw up lp in next sc, (YO, draw up lp in same sc) twice; sk next sc, YO, draw up lp in next sc, YO and draw through 2 lps on hook, YO and draw through all 8 lps on hook; ch 1, turn.

Row 5: Sc in next 10 sts; * 5 sc in next st; sc in next 9 sts, sk next st, sc in next 9 sts; rep from * across to last st; 3 sc in last st; ch 1, turn.

Rep Rows 2 through 5 for pattern.

#23

Multiple of 16 + 11

> **PATTERN STITCHES**
>
> **Cluster** (CL): Keeping last lp of each dc on hook, 3 dc in st, YO and draw through all 4 lps on hook: CL made.
>
> **2-dc Cluster** (2-dc CL): Keeping last lp of each dc on hook, 2 dc in st, YO and draw through all 3 lps on hook: 2-dc CL made.

Row 1 (right side): In 11th ch from hook work [CL (see Pattern Stitches), ch 3, CL]; * ch 3, sk next 3 chs, dc in next ch, ch 3, sk next 3 chs, sc in next ch, ch 3, sk next 3 chs, dc in next ch, ch 3, sk next 3 chs, in next ch work (CL, ch 3, CL); rep from * across to last ch; in last ch work (CL, ch 1, trc); ch 1, turn.

Row 2: Sc in next trc, ch 3; * dc in next dc, ch 3, 2-dc CL (see Pattern Stitches) in top of dc just made; CL in each of next 2 ch-3 lps; ch 3, 2-dc CL in top of last CL made; dc in next dc, ch 3, sk next ch-3 lp, sc in next ch-3 lp, ch 3; rep from * across to beg 10 skipped chs; dc in 7th ch of 10 skipped chs; ch 6, turn.

Row 3: Sc in next sc; * ch 3, dc in next dc, ch 3, between next 2 CLs work (CL, ch 3, CL); ch 3, dc in next dc, ch 3, sc in next sc; rep from * across; ch 4, turn.

Row 4: CL in next ch-3 lp; ch 3, 2-dc CL in top of CL just made; dc in next dc; * ch 3, sk next ch-3 lp, sc in next ch-3 lp, ch 3, dc in next dc, ch 3, 2-dc CL in top of dc just made; CL in each of next 2 ch-3 lps; ch 3, 2-dc CL in top of last CL made; dc in next dc; rep from * across to turning ch; dc in 3rd ch of turning ch-6; ch 6, turn.

Row 5: * Between next 2 CLs work (CL, ch 3, CL); ch 3, dc in next dc, ch 3, sc in next sc, ch 3, dc in next dc, ch 3; rep from * across to last CL; in last CL work (CL, ch 1, trc); ch 1, turn.

Row 6: Sc in next trc, ch 3; * dc in next dc, ch 3, 2-dc CL in top of dc just made; CL in each of next 2 ch-3 lps; ch 3, 2-dc CL in top of last CL made; dc in next dc, ch 3, sk next ch-3 lp, sc in next ch-3 lp, ch 3; rep from * across to turning ch; dc in 3rd ch of turning ch-6; ch 6, turn.

Rep Rows 3 through 6 for pattern.

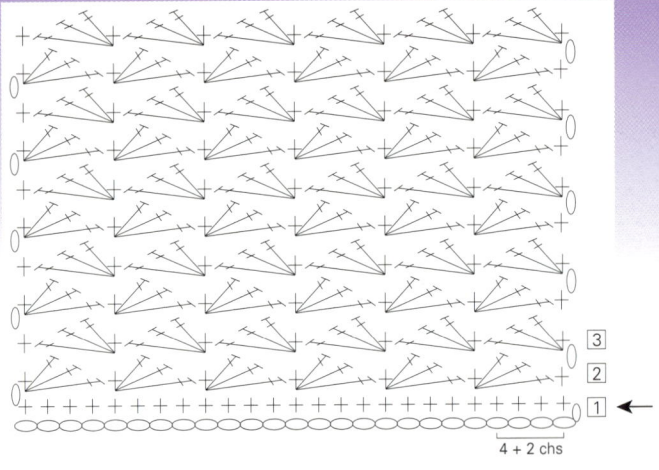

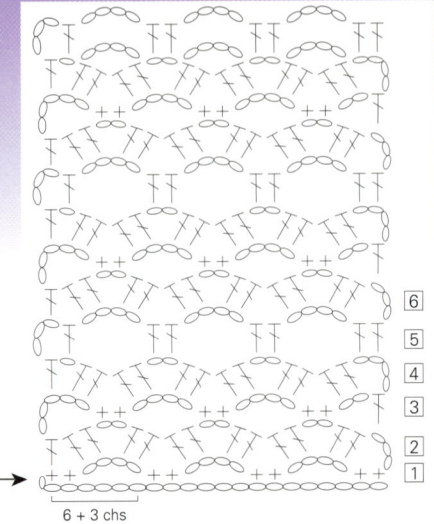

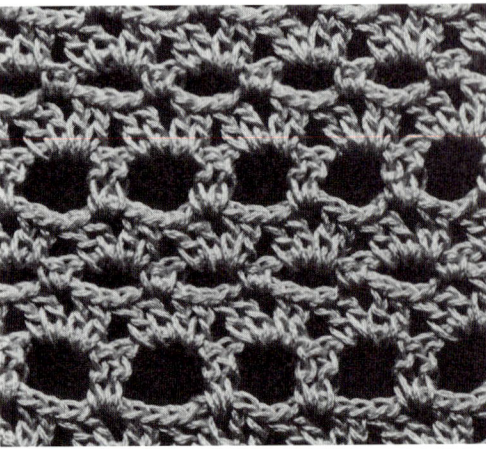

#24

Multiple of 4 + 2

Row 1 (right side): Sc in 2nd ch from hook, and in each rem ch; ch 1, turn.

Row 2: In next sc work (sc, 3 dc); * sk next 3 sc, in next sc work (sc, 3 dc); rep from * across to last 4 sc; sk next 3 sc, sc in last sc; ch 1, turn.

Row 3: In next sc work (sc, 3 dc); * sk next 3 dc, in next sc work (sc, 3 dc); rep from * across to last sc; sc in last sc; ch 1, turn.

Rep Row 3 for pattern.

#25

Multiple of 6 + 3

Row 1: Sc in 2nd ch from hook and in next ch; * ch 4, sk next 4 chs, sc in next 2 chs; rep from * across; ch 3, turn.

Row 2 (right side): * In next ch-4 lp work (2 dc, ch 2, 2 dc); rep from * across to last 2 sc; sk next sc, dc in last sc; ch 5, turn.

Row 3: 2 sc in next ch-2 sp; * ch 4, 2 sc in next ch-2 sp; rep from * across to turning ch; ch 2, dc in 3rd ch of turning ch-3; ch 4, turn.

Row 4: 2 dc in next ch-2 sp; * in next ch-4 lp work (2 dc, ch 2, 2 dc); rep from * across to turning ch lp; 2 dc in lp; ch 1, dc in 3rd ch of turning ch-5; ch 3, turn.

Row 5: Dc in next ch-1 sp, ch 4; * 2 dc in next ch-2 sp; ch 4; rep from * across to turning ch; dc in next 2 chs of turning ch-4; ch 3, turn.

Row 6: * In next ch-4 lp work (2 dc, ch 2, 2 dc); rep from * across to last dc; sk last dc, dc in 3rd ch of turning ch-3; ch 5, turn.

Rep Rows 3 through 6 for pattern.

#26

Multiple of 6 + 2

> **PATTERN STITCH**
>
> **Cluster** (CL): YO, draw up lp in next st, (YO, draw up lp in same st) twice; YO and draw through all 7 lps on hook: CL made.

Row 1 (right side): Sc in 2nd ch from hook, sk next 2 chs, in next ch work [CL (see Pattern Stitch), ch 2, CL, ch 2, CL]; ch 1, sk next 2 chs, sc in next ch, sk next 2 chs; * in next ch work (CL, ch 2, CL, ch 2, CL); ch 1, sk next 2 chs, sc in next ch, sk next 2 chs; rep from * across to last ch; sc in last ch; ch 3, turn.

Row 2: Dc in first sc, ch 2, sk next CL, sc in next CL, ch 2; * 3 dc in next sc; ch 2, sk next CL, sc in next CL, ch 2; rep from * across to last sc; 2 dc in last sc; ch 4, turn.

Row 3: CL in first dc; ch 1, sc in next sc; * in 2nd dc of next 3-dc group work (CL, ch 2, CL, ch 2, CL); ch 1, sc in next sc; rep from * across to turning ch; in 3rd ch of turning ch-3 work (CL, ch 2, dc); ch 1, turn.

Row 4: Sc in next dc, ch 2, 3 dc in next sc; ch 2; * sk next CL, sc in next CL, ch 2, 3 dc in next sc; ch 2; rep from * across to turning ch lp; sc in lp; ch 1, turn.

Row 5: Sc in next sc; * in 2nd dc of next 3-dc group work (CL, ch 2, CL, ch 2, CL); ch 1, sc in next sc; rep from * across; ch 3, turn.

Rep Rows 2 through 5 for pattern.

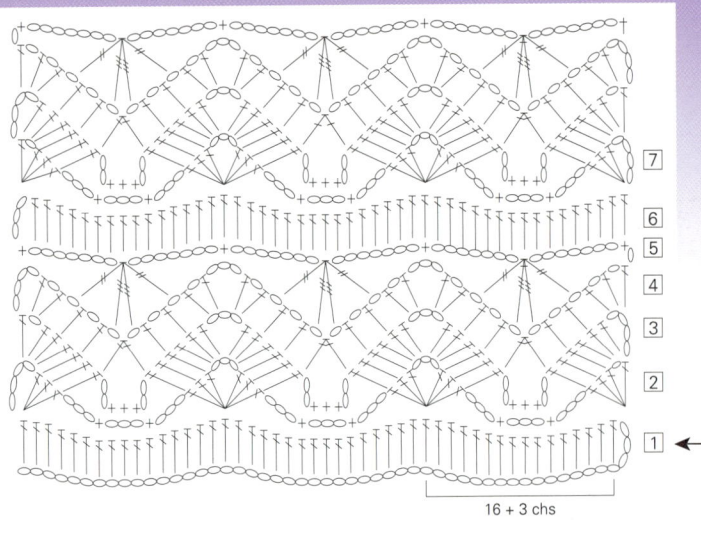

16 + 3 chs

#27

Multiple of 16 + 4

PATTERN STITCHES

Double Triple Crochet (dtrc): YO 3 times; draw up lp in next st, (YO and draw through 2 lps on hook) 4 times: dtrc made.

Cluster (CL): Keeping last lp of each dc on hook, dc in next dc, sk next 3 sc, dc in next dc, YO and draw through all 3 lps on hook: CL made.

4-st Cluster (4-st CL): Keeping last lp of each st on hook, trc in next ch-1 sp, sk next ch-1 sp, dtrc in each of next 2 ch-1 sps, sk next ch-1 sp, trc in next ch-1 sp, YO and draw through all 5 lps on hook: 4-st CL made.

Row 1 (right side): Dc in 4th ch from hook and in each rem ch; ch 4, turn.

Row 2: 3 dc in first dc, ch 3, sk next 5 dc, sc in next dc, ch 3, sk next 3 dc, sc in next dc; * ch 3, sk next 5 dc, in next dc work (3 dc, ch 3, 3 dc); ch 3, sk next 5 dc, sc in next dc, ch 3, sk next 3 dc, sc in next dc; rep from * across to last 5 dc; ch 3, sk next 5 dc, in 3rd ch of beg 3 skipped chs work (3 dc, ch 1, dc); ch 4, turn.

Row 3: 3 dc in next ch-1 sp; dc in next 3 dc, ch 2, sk next ch-3 lp, 3 sc in next ch-3 lp; ch 2; * dc in next 3 dc, in next ch-3 lp work (3 dc, ch 3, 3 dc); dc in next 3 dc, ch 2, sk next ch-3 lp, 3 sc in next ch-3 lp; ch 2; rep from * across to turning ch; 3 dc in turning ch lp; ch 1, dc in 3rd ch of turning ch-4; ch 4, turn.

Row 4: In next ch-1 sp work (dc, ch 1, dc); ch 1, (sk next dc, dc in next dc, ch 1) twice; sk next dc, CL (see Pattern Stitches) over next 5 sts; (ch 1, sk next dc, dc in next dc) twice; * ch 1, sk next dc, in next ch-3 lp work (dc, ch 1, dc, ch 3, dc, ch 1, dc); ch 1, (sk next dc, dc in next dc, ch 1) twice; sk next dc, CL over next 5 sts; (ch 1, sk next dc, dc in next dc) twice; rep from * across to turning ch lp; ch 1, in lp work (dc, ch 1, dc); ch 1, dc in 3rd ch of turning ch-4; ch 1, turn.

Row 5: Sc in next dc, ch 7, sk next 2 ch-1 sps, 4-st CL (see Pattern Stitches) over next 6 ch-1 sps; * ch 7, sc in next ch-3 lp, ch 7, sk next ch-1 sp, 4-st CL over next 6 ch-1 sps; rep from * across to turning ch; ch 7, sc in 3rd ch of turning ch-4; ch 3, turn.

Row 6: 7 dc in next ch-7 lp; dc in next 4-st CL, 7 dc in next ch-7 lp; dc in next sc; * 7 dc in next ch-7 lp; dc in next 4-st CL, 7 dc in next ch-7 lp; dc in next sc; rep from * across; ch 4, turn.

Row 7: 3 dc in first dc, ch 3, sk next 5 dc, sc in next dc, ch 3, sk next 3 dc, sc in next dc; * ch 3, sk next 5 dc, in next dc work (3 dc, ch 3, 3 dc); ch 3, sk next 5 dc, sc in next dc, ch 3, sk next 3 dc, sc in next dc; rep from * across to last 5 dc; ch 3, sk next 5 dc, in 3rd ch of turning ch-3 work (3 dc, ch 1, dc); ch 4, turn.

Rep Rows 3 through 7 for pattern.

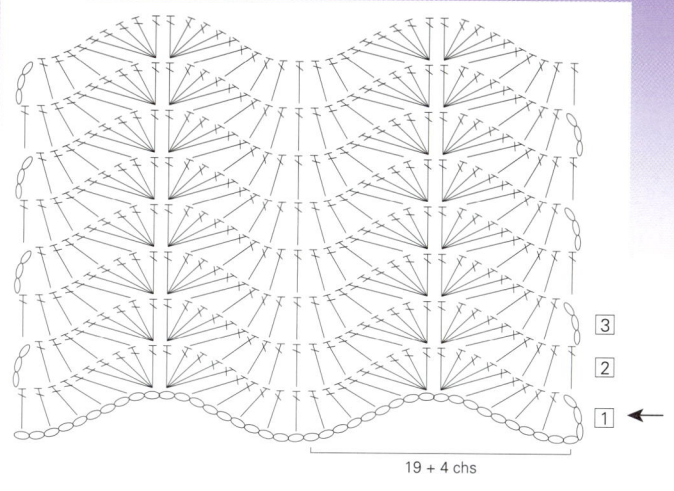

19 + 4 chs

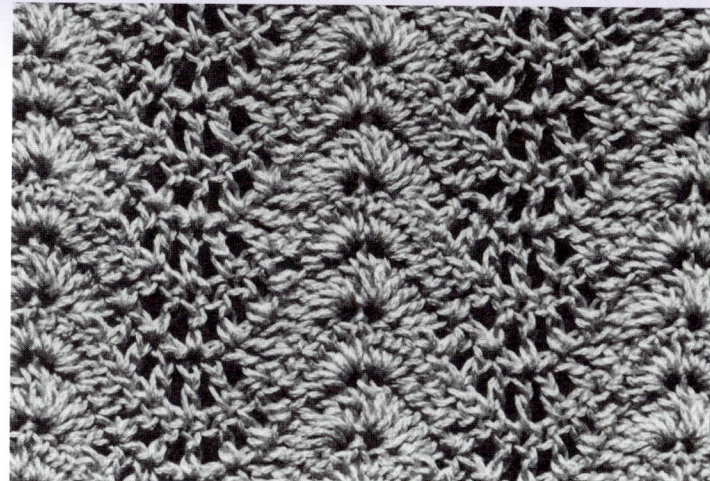

#28

Multiple of 19 + 4

Row 1 (right side): Dc in 6th ch from hook, (sk next ch, dc in next ch) 3 times; 5 dc in each of next 2 chs; dc in next ch; * (sk next ch, dc in next ch) 8 times; 5 dc in each of next 2 chs; dc in next dc; rep from * across to last 8 chs; (sk next ch, dc in next ch) 4 times; ch 3 (counts as first dc on following rows), turn.

Row 2: (Sk next dc, dc in next dc) 4 times; 5 dc in each of next 2 dc; dc in next dc; * (sk next dc, dc in next dc) 8 times; 5 dc in each of next 2 dc; dc in next dc; rep from * across to last 7 dc; (sk next dc, dc in next dc) 3 times; sk next dc, dc in 5th ch of beg 5 skipped chs; ch 3, turn.

Row 3: (Sk next dc, dc in next dc) 4 times; 5 dc in each of next 2 dc; dc in next dc; * (sk next dc, dc in next dc) 8 times; 5 dc in each of next 2 dc; dc in next dc; rep from * across to last 7 dc; (sk next dc, dc in next dc) 3 times; sk next dc, dc in 3rd ch of turning ch-3; ch 3, turn.

Rep Row 3 for pattern.

#29

Multiple of 35 + 7

> **PATTERN STITCH**
>
> **Popcorn** (PC): 5 dc in next st, drop lp from hook, insert hook in first dc made and draw dropped lp through, ch 1: PC made.

Row 1 (right side): Sc in 2nd ch from hook; * ch 5, sk next 4 chs, sc in next ch; rep from * across; ch 5, turn.

Row 2: (Sc in next ch-5 lp, ch 5) 3 times; * sc in next ch-5 lp, 5 dc in next sc; (sc in next ch-5 lp, ch 5) 6 times; rep from * across to last ch-5 lp; sc in last ch-5 lp, ch 2, dc in last sc; ch 1, turn.

Row 3: Sc in next dc, (ch 5, sc in next ch-5 lp) 3 times; * 5 dc in next sc; sk next 2 dc, sc in next dc, 5 dc in next sc; (sc in next ch-5 lp, ch 5) 5 times; sc in next ch-5 lp; rep from * across to last 3 ch-5 lps; (sc in next ch-5 lp, ch 5) 3 times; sc in 3rd ch of turning ch-5; ch 5, turn.

Row 4: (Sc in next ch-5 lp, ch 5) twice; * sc in next ch-5 lp, 5 dc in next sc; sk next 2 dc, sc in next dc, ch 5, sk next 5 sts, sc in next dc, 5 dc in next sc; (sc in next ch-5 lp, ch 5) 4 times; rep from * across to last 3 ch-5 lps; (sc in next ch-5 lp, ch 5) twice; sc in next ch-5 lp, ch 2, dc in next sc; ch 1, turn.

Row 5: Sc in next dc, (ch 5, sc in next ch-5 lp) twice; * 5 dc in next sc; sk next 2 dc, sc in next dc, ch 5, sc in next ch-5 lp, ch 5, sk next 2 dc, sc in next dc, 5 dc in next sc; (sc in next ch-5 lp, ch 5) 3 times; sc in next ch-5 lp; rep from * across to last 2 ch-5 lps; (sc in next ch-5 lp, ch 5) twice; sc in 3rd ch of turning ch-5; ch 5, turn.

Row 6: Sc in next ch-5 lp, ch 5; * sc in next ch-5 lp, 5 dc in next sc; sk next 2 dc, sc in next dc, ch 5, sc in next ch-5 lp, in next sc work (2 dc, ch 3, 2 dc); sc in next ch-5 lp, ch 5, sk next 2 dc, sc in next dc, 5 dc in next sc; (sc in next ch-5 lp, ch 5) twice; rep from * across to last 2 ch-5 lps; sc in next ch-5 lp, ch 5, sc in next ch-5 lp, ch 2, dc in next sc; ch 1, turn.

Row 7: Sc in next dc, ch 5, sc in next ch-5 lp; * ch 5, sk next 2 dc, sc in next dc, ch 5, sc in next ch-5 lp, ch 2, 7 dc in next ch-3 lp; ch 2, sc in next ch-5 lp, ch 5, sk next 2 dc, sc in next dc, (ch 5, sc in next ch-5 lp) twice; rep from * across to turning ch; ch 5, sc in 3rd ch of turning ch-5; ch 5, turn.

Row 8: (Sc in next ch-5 lp, ch 5) twice; * sc in next ch-5 lp, ch 2, 2 dc in each of next 3 dc; dc in next dc, 2 dc in each of next 3 dc; ch 2, (sc in next ch-5 lp, ch 5) 4 times; rep from * across to last 3 ch-5 lps; (sc in next ch-5 lp, ch 5) twice; sc in next ch-5 lp, ch 2, dc in next sc; ch 1, turn.

Row 9: Sc in next dc, (ch 5, sc in next ch-5 lp) twice; * ch 2, [PC (see Pattern Stitch) in next dc, ch 3, sk next dc] 6 times; PC in next dc; ch 2, (sc in next ch-5 lp, ch 5) 3 times; sc in next ch-5 lp; rep from * across to last 2 ch-5 lps; (sc in next ch-5 lp, ch 5) twice; sc in 3rd ch of turning ch-5; ch 5, turn.

Row 10: (Sc in next ch-5 lp, ch 5) twice; * sc in next ch-3 lp, ch 5, sk next ch-3 lp, sc in next ch-3 lp, ch 5, sc in next ch-3 lp, ch 5, sk next ch-3 lp, sc in next ch-3 lp, (ch 5, sc in next ch-5 lp) 3 times; ch 5; rep from * across to last 2 ch-5 lps; (ch 5, sc in next ch-5 lp) twice; ch 2, dc in next sc; ch 1, turn.

Row 11: Sc in next dc; * ch 5, sc in next ch-5 lp; rep from * across to turning ch; ch 5, sc in 3rd ch of turning ch-5; ch 5, turn.

Rep Rows 2 through 11 for pattern.

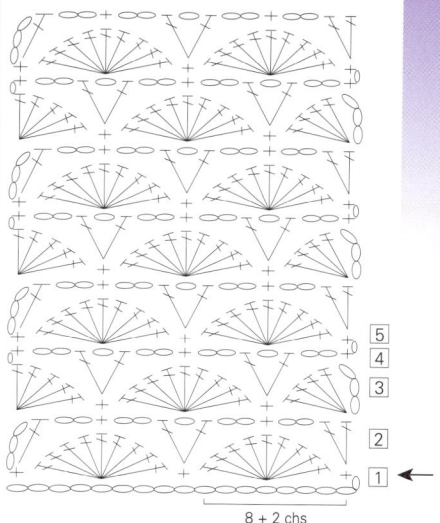

8 + 2 chs

#30

Multiple of 8 + 2

Row 1 (right side): Sc in 2nd ch from hook; * sk next 3 chs, 9 dc in next ch; sk next 3 chs, sc in next ch; rep from * across; ch 3, turn.

Row 2: Dc in first sc; * ch 2, sk next 4 dc, sc in next dc, ch 2, in next sc work (dc, ch 1, dc); rep from * across to last sc; 2 dc in last sc; ch 3, turn.

Row 3: 4 dc in first dc; * sc in next sc, 9 dc in next ch-1 sp; rep from * across to turning ch; 5 dc in 3rd ch of turning ch-3; ch 1, turn.

Row 4: * Sc in next dc, ch 2, in next sc work (dc, ch 1, dc); ch 2, sk next 4 dc; rep from * across to turning ch; sc in 3rd ch of turning ch-3; ch 1, turn.

Row 5: * Sc in next sc, 9 dc in next ch-1 sp; rep from * across to last sc; sc in last sc; ch 3, turn.

Rep Rows 2 through 5 for pattern.

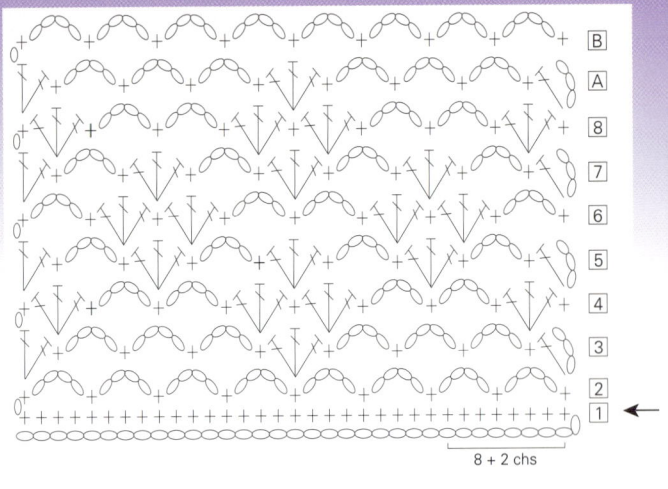
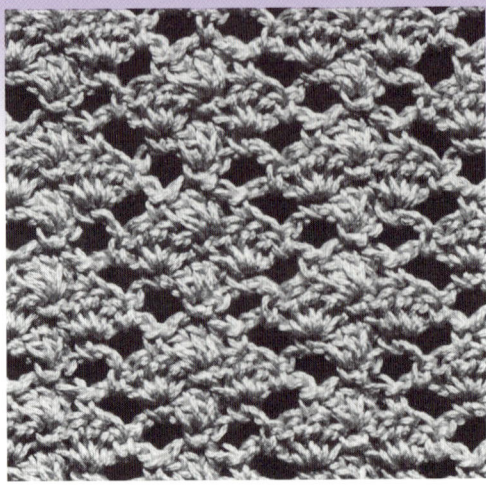

#31

Multiple of 8 + 2

Row 1 (right side): Sc in 2nd ch from hook and in each rem ch across; ch 1, turn.

Row 2: Sc in next sc; * ch 4, sk next 3 sc, sc in next sc; rep from * across; ch 3, turn.

Row 3: Dc in first sc, sc in next ch-4 lp, (ch 4, sc in next ch-4 lp) 3 times; * 3 dc in next sc; sc in next ch-4 lp, (ch 4, sc in next ch-4 lp) 3 times; rep from * across to last sc; 2 dc in last sc; ch 1, turn.

Row 4: Sc in next dc, 3 dc in next sc; * sc in next ch-4 lp, (ch 4, sc in next ch-4 lp) twice; 3 dc in next sc; sk next dc, sc in next dc, 3 dc in next sc; rep from * across to turning ch; sc in 3rd ch of turning ch-3; ch 3, turn.

Row 5: Dc in next sc; * sk next dc, sc in next dc, ch 4, sc in next ch-4 lp, 3 dc in next sc; sc in next ch-4 lp, ch 4, sk next dc, sc in next dc, 3 dc in next sc; rep from * across, ending last rep without working last dc; ch 1, turn.

Row 6: Sc in next dc; * ch 4, sc in next ch-4 lp, 3 dc in next sc; sk next dc, sc in next dc, 3 dc in next sc; sc in next ch-4 lp, ch 4, sk next dc, sc in next dc; rep from * across to turning ch; sc in 3rd ch of turning ch-3; ch 3, turn.

Row 7: Dc in first sc; * sc in next ch-4 lp, ch 4, sk next dc, sc in next dc, 3 dc in next sc; sk next dc, sc in next dc, ch 4, sc in next ch-4 lp, 3 dc in next sc; rep from * across, ending last rep without working last dc; ch 1, turn.

Row 8: Sc in next dc; * 3 dc in next sc; sc in next ch-4 lp, ch 4, sk next dc, sc in next dc, ch 4, sc in next ch-4 lp, 3 dc in next sc; sk next dc, sc in next dc; rep from * across to turning ch; sc in 3rd ch of turning ch-3; ch 3, turn.

Rep Rows 5 through 8 for patt until desired length, then work following 2 rows:

Row A: Dc in first sc; * sk next dc, sc in next dc, (ch 4, sc in next ch-4 lp) twice; ch 4, sk next dc, sc in next dc, 3 dc in next sc; rep from * across, ending last rep without working last dc; ch 1, turn.

Row B: Sc in next dc; * (ch 4, sc in next ch-4 lp) 3 times; ch 4, sk next dc, sc in next dc; rep from * across to turning ch; sc in 3rd ch of turning ch-3. Finish off.

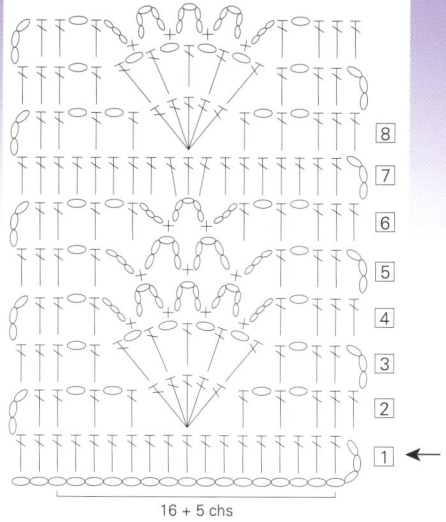

16 + 5 chs

#32

Multiple of 16 + 5

Row 1 (right side): Dc in 4th ch from hook and in each rem ch; ch 3 (counts as a dc on this and following rows), turn.

Row 2: Dc in next 2 dc; * (ch 1, sk next dc, dc in next dc) twice; sk next 2 dc, 5 dc in next dc; sk next 2 dc, (dc in next dc, ch 1, sk next dc) twice; dc in next 3 dc; rep from * across to beg 3 skipped chs; dc in 3rd ch of 3 skipped chs; ch 3, turn.

Row 3: Dc in next 2 dc; * ch 1, dc in next dc, sk next dc, (dc in next dc, ch 1) 4 times; dc in next dc, sk next dc, dc in next dc, ch 1, dc in next 3 dc; rep from * across to turning ch; dc in 3rd ch of turning ch-3; ch 3, turn.

Row 4: Dc in next 2 dc; * ch 1, dc in next dc, ch 3, sc in next ch-1 sp, (ch 5, sc in next ch-1 sp) 3 times; ch 3, sk next dc, dc in next dc, ch 1, dc in next 3 dc; rep from * across to turning ch; dc in 3rd ch of turning ch-3; ch 3, turn.

Row 5: Dc in next 2 dc; * ch 1, dc in next dc, ch 3, sc in next ch-5 lp, (ch 5, sc in next ch-5 lp) twice; ch 3, dc in next dc, ch 1, dc in next 3 dc; rep from * across to turning ch; ch 3, turn.

Row 6: Dc in next 2 dc; * ch 1, dc in next dc, ch 1, dc in next ch-3 lp, ch 3, sc in next ch-5 lp, ch 5, sc in next ch-5 lp, ch 3, dc in next ch-3 lp, ch 1, dc in next dc, ch 1, dc in next 3 dc; rep from * across to turning ch; dc in 3rd ch of turning ch-3; ch 3, turn.

Row 7: Dc in next 2 dc; * dc in next ch-1 sp, in next dc, in next ch-1 sp, in next dc, and in next ch-3 lp; 3 dc in next ch-5 lp; dc in next ch-3 lp, in next dc, in next ch-1 sp, in next dc, in next ch-1 sp, and in next 3 dc; rep from * across to turning ch; dc in 3rd ch of turning ch-3; ch 3, turn.

Row 8: Dc in next 2 dc; * (ch 1, sk next dc, dc in next dc) twice; sk next 2 dc, 5 dc in next dc; sk next 2 dc, (dc in next dc, ch 1, sk next dc) twice; dc in next 3 dc; rep from * across to turning ch; dc in 3rd ch of turning ch-3; ch 3, turn.

Rep Rows 3 through 8 for pattern.

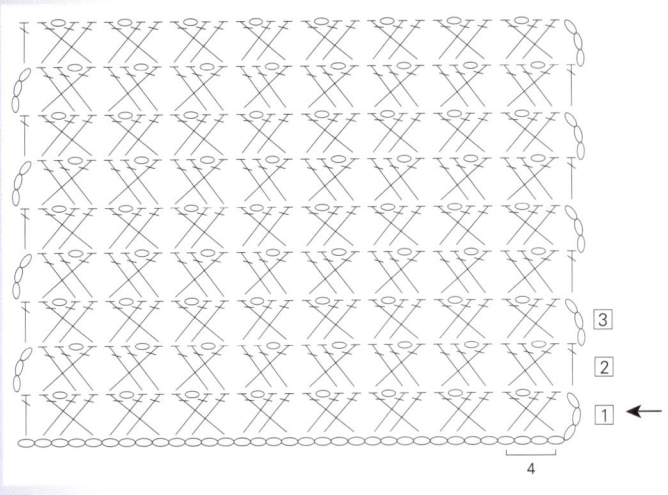

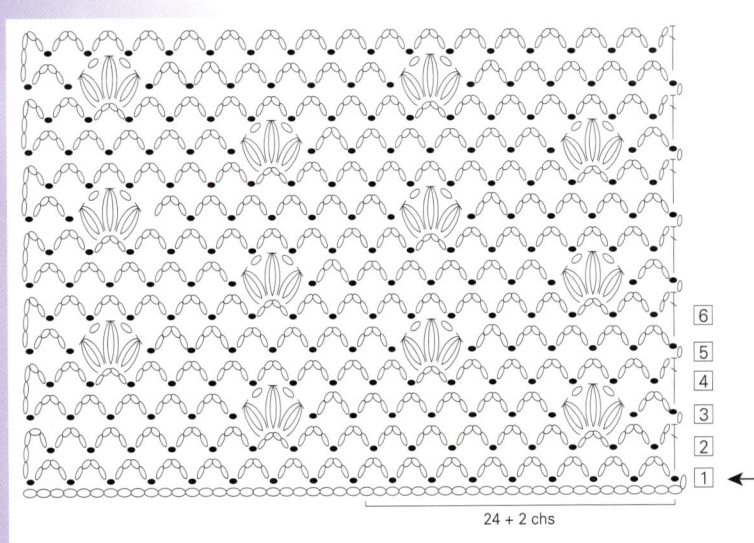

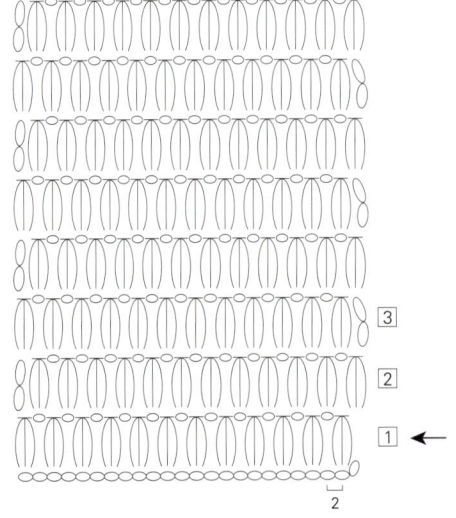

#33

Multiple of 4

Row 1 (right side): Dc in 6th and 7th chs from hook, ch 1, dc in 4th ch from hook; * sk next 2 chs, dc in next 2 chs, ch 1, dc in first skipped ch; rep from * across to last ch; dc in last ch; ch 3 (counts as first dc on following rows), turn.

Row 2: * Sk next dc and next ch-1 sp, dc in next 2 dc, ch 1, dc in skipped dc; rep from * across to beg 3 skipped chs; dc in 3rd ch of 3 skipped chs; ch 3, turn.

Row 3: * Sk next dc and next ch-1 sp, dc in next 2 dc, ch 1, dc in skipped dc; rep from * across to turning ch; dc in 3rd ch of turning ch-3; ch 3, turn.

Rep Row 3 for pattern.

#34

Multiple of 24 + 2

> **PATTERN STITCH**
>
> **Cluster** (CL): (YO, draw up lp in next lp) 4 times; YO and draw through all 9 lps on hook: CL made.

Row 1 (right side): Sl st in 2nd ch from hook; * ch 4, sk next 2 chs, sl st in next ch; rep from * across; ch 5, turn.

Row 2: * Sl st in next ch-4 lp; ch 4; rep from * across to last sl st; ch 2, dc in last sl st; ch 1, turn.

Row 3: Sl st in next dc; ch 4; * sl st in next ch-4 lp; in next ch-4 lp work [CL (see Pattern Stitch), ch 1, CL, ch 1, CL]; (sl st in next ch-4 lp, ch 4) 6 times; rep from * across to turning ch; sl st in 3rd ch of turning ch-5; ch 5, turn.

Row 4: (Sl st in next ch-4 lp, ch 4) 5 times; * (sl st in next ch-1 sp, ch 4) twice; (sl st in next ch-4 lp, ch 4) 6 times; rep from * across to last ch-4 lp; sl st in last ch-4 lp; ch 2, dc in last sl st; ch 1, turn.

Row 5: Sl st in next dc; (ch 4, sl st in next ch-4 lp) 5 times; * in next ch-4 lp work (CL, ch 1, CL, ch 1, CL); (sl st in next ch-4 lp, ch 4) 6 times; sl st in next ch-4 lp; rep from * across to last ch-4 lp; sl st in last ch-4 lp; ch 4, sl st in 3rd ch of turning ch-5; ch 5, turn.

Row 6: Sl st in next ch-4 lp; ch 4; * (sl st in next ch-1 sp, ch 4) twice; (sl st in next ch-4 lp, ch 4) 6 times; rep from * across to last ch-4 lp; sl st in last ch-4 lp; ch 2, dc in last sl st; ch 1, turn.

Rep Rows 3 through 6 for pattern.

#35

Multiple of 2

> **PATTERN STITCH**
>
> **Cluster** (CL): YO, draw up lp in next st, (YO, draw up lp in same st) twice; YO and draw through all 7 lps on hook: CL made.

Row 1 (right side): CL (see Pattern Stitch) in 2nd ch from hook; * ch 1, sk next ch, CL in next ch; rep from * across; ch 2, turn.

Row 2: CL in next ch-1 sp; * ch 1, CL in next ch-1 sp; rep from * across to beg skipped ch; ch 1, CL in beg skipped ch; ch 2, turn.

Row 3: CL in next ch-1 sp; * ch 1, CL in next ch-1 sp; rep from * across to turning ch lp; ch 1, CL in lp; ch 2, turn.

Rep Row 3 for pattern.

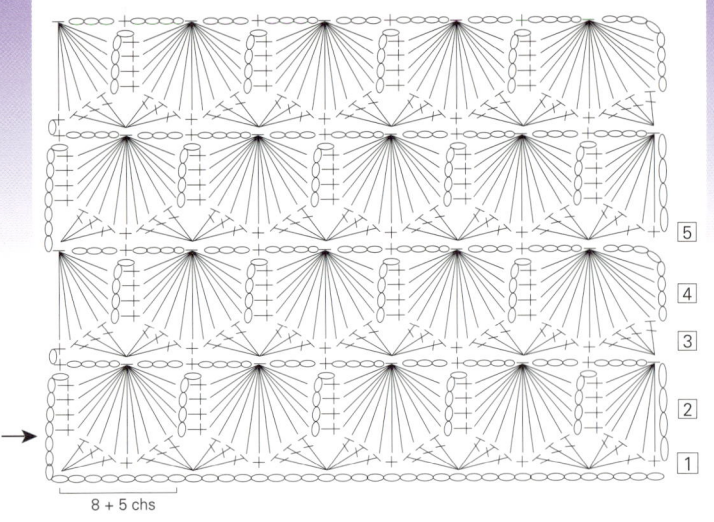

8 + 5 chs

#36

Multiple of 8 + 5

PATTERN STITCHES

Beg Cluster (beg CL): YO, draw up lp in next sc, (YO, draw up lp in next dc) 3 times; (YO, draw up lp in next sc) 4 times; YO and draw through all 17 lps on hook: beg CL made.

Cluster (CL): Working in unused lps of next 4 chs, (YO, draw up lp in next lp) 4 times; (YO, draw up lp in next dc) 3 times; YO, draw up lp in next sc, (YO, draw up lp in next dc) 3 times; (YO, draw up lp in next sc) 4 times; YO and draw through all 31 lps on hook: CL made.

Half Cluster (half CL): Working in unused lps of next 4 chs, (YO, draw up lp in next lp) 4 times; (YO, draw up lp in next dc) 3 times; YO, draw up lp in next sc, YO and draw through all 17 lps on hook: half CL made.

Row 1: Sc in 2nd ch from hook and in next 3 chs, sk next 3 chs, 3 dc in next ch; sk next 3 chs, sc in next ch; * sk next 3 chs, in next ch work (3 dc, ch 5, sc in 2nd ch from hook and in next 3 chs, 3 dc); sk next 3 chs, sc in next ch; rep from * across; ch 4, turn.

Row 2 (right side): Beg CL (see Pattern Stitches) over next 8 sts; * ch 4, sc in skipped ch of next ch 5, ch 3; CL (see Pattern Stitches) over next 15 sts; rep from * across to beg skipped ch; ch 4, sc in skipped ch; ch 1, turn.

Row 3: Sc in next sc; * in next CL work (3 dc, ch 5, sc in 2nd ch from hook and in next 3 chs, 3 dc); sc in next sc; rep from * across to beg CL; 4 dc in beg CL; ch 8, turn.

Row 4: Beg in 5th ch from hook, CL over next 4 chs, next 4 dc, next sc, next 3 dc, and next 4 sc; ch 4, sc in skipped ch of next ch 5, ch 3; * CL; ch 4, sc in skipped ch of next ch 5, ch 3; rep from * across to last ch 5; sc in skipped ch of last ch 5, half CL (see Pattern Stitches); ch 8, turn.

Row 5: Sc in 2nd ch from hook and in next 3 chs, 3 dc in next half CL; sc in next sc; * in next CL work (3 dc, ch 5, sc in 2nd ch from hook and in next 3 chs, 3 dc); sc in next sc; rep from * across to turning ch; sc in 5th ch of turning ch-8; ch 4, turn.

Rep Rows 2 through 5 for pattern.

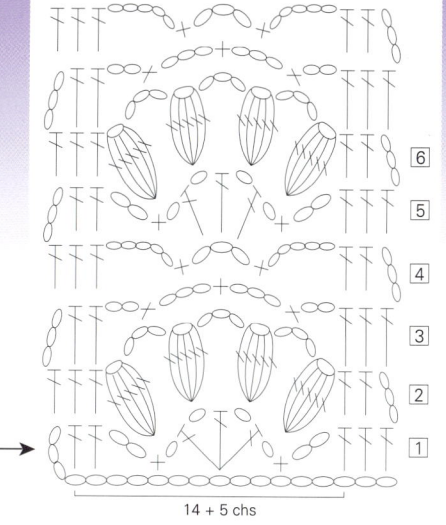

14 + 5 chs

#37

Multiple of 14 + 5

> **PATTERN STITCH**
>
> **Popcorn** (PC): 5 dc in next sp, drop lp from hook, insert hook in first dc made, draw dropped lp through, ch 1: PC made.

Row 1: Dc in 4th ch from hook and in next ch; * ch 2, sk next 2 chs, sc in next ch, ch 1, sk next 2 chs, in next ch work (dc, ch 1) 3 times; sk next 2 chs, sc in next ch, ch 2, sk next 2 chs, dc in next 3 chs; rep from * across; ch 3 (counts as first dc on following rows), turn.

Row 2 (right side): Dc in next 2 dc; * [PC (see Pattern Stitch) in next ch-1 sp; ch 3] 3 times; PC in next ch-1 sp; dc in next 3 dc; rep from * across to beg 3 skipped chs; dc in 3rd ch of 3 skipped chs; ch 3, turn.

Row 3: Dc in next 2 dc; * ch 2, sc in next ch-3 lp, (ch 3, sc in next ch-3 lp) twice; ch 2, dc in next 3 dc; rep from * across to turning ch; dc in 3rd ch of turning ch-3; ch 3, turn.

Row 4: Dc in next 2 dc; * ch 5, sc in next ch-3 lp, ch 3, sc in next ch-3 lp, ch 5, dc in next 3 dc; rep from * across to turning ch; dc in 3rd ch of turning ch-3; ch 3, turn.

Row 5: Dc in next 2 dc; * ch 2, sc in next ch-5 lp, ch 1, in next ch-3 lp work (dc, ch 1) 3 times; sc in next ch-5 lp, ch 2, dc in next 3 dc; rep from * across to turning ch; dc in 3rd ch of turning ch-3; ch 3, turn.

Row 6: Dc in next 2 dc; * (PC in next ch-1 sp; ch 3) 3 times; PC in next ch-1 sp; dc in next 3 dc; rep from * across to turning ch; dc in 3rd ch of turning ch-3; ch 3, turn.

Rep Rows 3 through 6 for pattern.

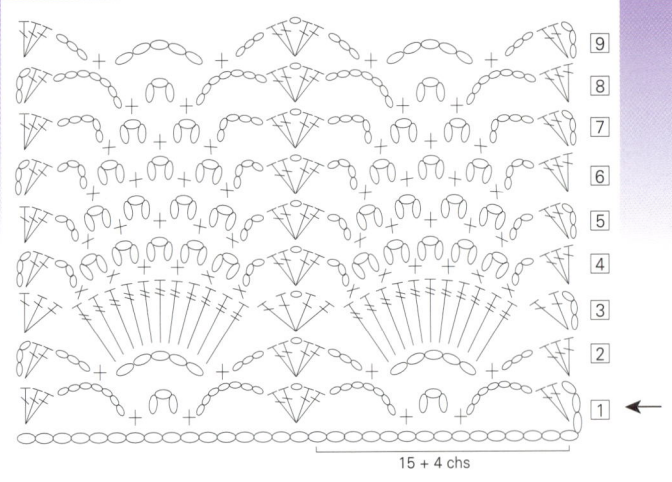

#38

Multiple of 15 + 4

Row 1 (right side): 2 dc in 4th ch from hook, ch 7, sk next 5 chs, sc in next ch, ch 3, sk next 2 chs, sc in next ch, ch 7, sk next 5 chs; * in next ch work (2 dc, ch 1, 2 dc): shell made; ch 7, sk next 5 chs, sc in next ch, ch 3, sk next 2 chs, sc in next ch, ch 7, sk next 5 chs; rep from * across to last ch; 3 dc in last ch; ch 3, turn.

Row 2: 2 dc in first dc, ch 3, sc in next ch-7 lp, ch 5, sc in next ch-7 lp, ch 3; * shell in ch-1 sp of next shell: shell in shell made; ch 3, sc in next ch-7 lp, ch 5, sc in next ch-7 lp, ch 3; rep from * across to beg 3 skipped chs; 3 dc in 3rd ch of 3 skipped chs; ch 3, turn.

Row 3: 2 dc in first dc, 11 trc in next ch-5 lp: pineapple base made; * shell in next shell; 11 trc in next ch-5 lp: pineapple base made; rep from * across to turning ch; 3 dc in 3rd ch of turning ch-3; ch 3, turn.

Row 4: 2 dc in first dc, ch 2, sc in next trc, (ch 3, sk next trc, sc in next trc) 5 times; ch 3; * shell in next shell; ch 3, sc in next trc, (ch 3, sk next trc, sc in next trc) 5 times; ch 3; rep from * across to turning ch; 3 dc in 3rd ch of turning ch-3; ch 3, turn.

Row 5: 2 dc in first dc, ch 3, sk next ch-3 lp, sc in next ch-3 lp, (ch 3, sc in next ch-3 lp) 4 times; ch 3; * shell in next shell; ch 3, sk next ch-3 lp, sc in next ch-3 lp, (ch 3, sc in next ch-3 lp) 4 times; ch 3; rep from * across to turning ch; 3 dc in 3rd ch of turning ch-3; ch 3, turn.

Row 6: 2 dc in first dc, ch 4, sk next ch-3 lp, sc in next ch-3 lp, (ch 3, sc in next ch-3 lp) 3 times; ch 4; * shell in next shell; ch 4, sk next ch-3 lp, sc in next ch-3 lp, (ch 3, sc in next ch-3 lp) 3 times; ch 4; rep from * across to turning ch; 3 dc in 3rd ch of turning ch-3; ch 3, turn.

Row 7: 2 dc in first dc, ch 5, sk next ch-4 lp, sc in next ch-3 lp, (ch 3, sc in next ch-3 lp) twice; ch 5; * shell in next shell; ch 5, sk next ch-4 lp, sc in next ch-3 lp, (ch 3, sc in next ch-3 lp) twice; ch 5; rep from * across to turning ch; 3 dc in 3rd ch of turning ch-3; ch 3, turn.

Row 8: 2 dc in first dc, ch 7, sk next ch-5 lp, sc in next ch-3 lp, ch 3, sc in next ch-3 lp, ch 7; * shell in next shell; ch 7, sk next ch-5 lp, sc in next ch-3 lp, ch 3, sc in next ch-3 lp, ch 7; rep from * across to turning ch; 3 dc in 3rd ch of turning ch-3; ch 3, turn.

Row 9: 2 dc in first dc, ch 3, sc in next ch-7 lp, ch 5, sc in next ch-7 lp, ch 3; * shell in next shell; ch 3, sc in next ch-7 lp, ch 5, sc in next ch-7 lp, ch 3; rep from * across to turning ch; 3 dc in 3rd ch of turning ch-3; ch 3, turn.

Rep Rows 3 through 9 for pattern.

16 + 10 chs

#39

Multiple of 16 + 10

Row 1 (right side): Sc in 2nd ch from hook, ch 5, sk next 3 chs, sc in next ch, ch 3, sl st in last sc made: picot made; * (ch 5, sk next 3 chs, sc in next ch) 4 times; ch 3, sl st in last sc made: picot made; rep from * across to last 4 chs; ch 5, sk next 3 chs, sc in last ch; ch 5, turn.

Row 2: * Sc in next ch-5 lp, ch 5; rep from * across to last ch-5 lp; sc in last ch-5 lp, ch 2, dc in last sc; ch 1, turn.

Row 3: Sc in next dc; * ch 5, sc in next ch-5 lp, picot; ch 5, sc in next ch-5 lp, 10 dc in next ch-5 lp; sc in next ch-5 lp; rep from * across to turning ch; ch 5, sc in 3rd ch of turning ch-5; ch 5, turn.

Row 4: * Sc in next ch-5 lp, ch 5, sc in next ch-5 lp, (dc in next dc, ch 1) 9 times; dc in next dc; rep from * across to last ch-5 lp; sc in last ch-5 lp, ch 2, dc in last sc; ch 1, turn.

Row 5: Sc in next dc; * ch 5, sc in next ch-5 lp, picot; ch 5, sk next ch-1 sp, sc in next ch-1 sp, (ch 5, sk next 2 ch-1 sps, sc in next ch-1 sp) twice; rep from * across to turning ch; sc in 3rd ch of turning ch-5; ch 5, turn.

Rep Rows 2 through 5 for pattern.

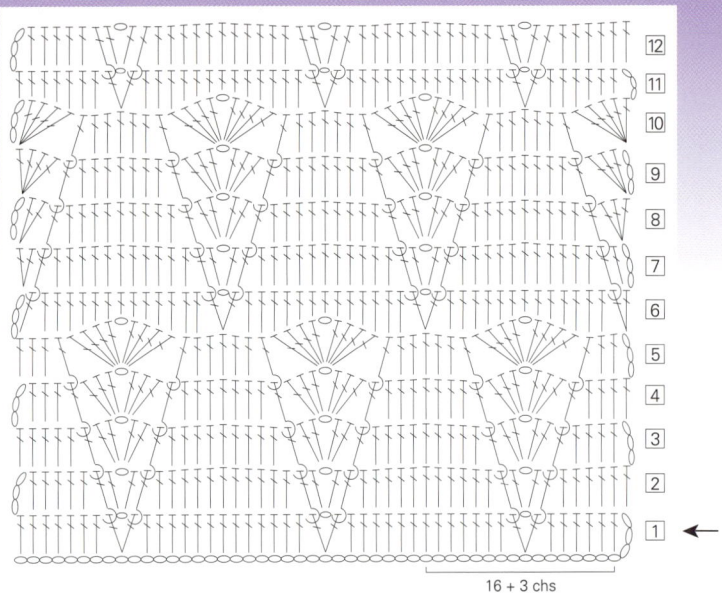

16 + 3 chs

#40

Multiple of 16 + 3

> **PATTERN STITCHES**
>
> **Front Post Double Crochet** (FPdc): YO, insert hook from front to back to front around post (see page 8) of next dc; YO and draw lp through, (YO and draw through 2 lps on hook) twice: FPdc made.
>
> **Back Post Double Crochet** (BPdc): YO, insert hook from back to front to back around post (see page 8) of next dc; YO and draw lp through, (YO and draw through 2 lps on hook) twice: BPdc made.

Row 1 (right side): Dc in 4th ch from hook and in next 5 chs; * sk next ch, in next ch work (dc, ch 1, dc); sk next ch, dc in next 13 chs; rep from * across to last 8 chs; sk next ch, dc in next 7 chs; ch 3 (counts as first dc on following rows), turn.

Row 2: Dc in next 5 dc; * sk next dc, BPdc (see Pattern Stitches) around next dc; in next ch-1 sp work (dc, ch 1, dc); BPdc around post of next dc; sk next dc, dc in next 11 dc; rep from * across to last 6 dc; sk next dc, dc in next 5 dc and in 3rd ch of beg 3 skipped chs; ch 3, turn.

Row 3: Dc in next 4 dc; * sk next dc, FPdc (see Pattern Stitches) around next BPdc; in next ch-1 sp work (2 dc, ch 1, 2 dc); FPdc around next BPdc; sk next dc, dc in next 9 dc; rep from * across to last 5 dc; sk next dc, dc in next 4 dc and in 3rd ch of turning ch-3; ch 3, turn.

Row 4: Dc in next 3 dc; * sk next dc, BPdc around next FPdc; in next ch-1 sp work (3 dc, ch 1, 3 dc); BPdc around next FPdc; sk next dc, dc in next 7 dc; rep from * across to last 5 dc; sk next dc, dc in next 3 dc and in 3rd ch of turning ch-3; ch 3, turn.

Row 5: Dc in next 2 dc; * sk next dc, FPdc around next BPdc; in next ch-1 sp work (4 dc, ch 1, 4 dc); FPdc around next BPdc; sk next dc, dc in next 5 dc; rep from * across to last 3 dc; sk next dc, dc in next 2 dc and in 3rd ch of turning ch-3; ch 3, turn.

Row 6: Dc in first dc; * sk next dc, dc in next 6 dc, in next ch-1 sp, and in next 6 dc; sk next dc, in next dc work (dc, ch 1, dc); rep from * across to last dc; sk last dc, 2 dc in 3rd ch of turning ch-3; ch 3, turn.

Row 7: Dc in first dc; * FPdc around next dc; sk next dc, dc in next 11 dc, sk next dc, FPdc around next dc; in next ch-1 sp work (dc, ch 1, dc); rep from * across to last dc; FPdc around last dc; 2 dc in 3rd ch of turning ch-3; ch 3, turn.

Row 8: 2 dc in first dc; * BPdc around next FPdc; sk next dc, dc in next 9 dc, sk next dc, BPdc around next FPdc; in next ch-1 sp work (2 dc, ch 1, 2 dc); rep from * across to turning ch; 3 dc in 3rd ch of turning ch-3; ch 3, turn.

Row 9: 3 dc in first dc; * sk next 2 dc, FPdc around next BPdc; sk next dc, dc in next 7 dc, FPdc around next BPdc; in next ch-1 sp work (3 dc, ch 1, 3 dc); rep from * across to turning ch; 4 dc in 3rd ch of turning ch-3; ch 3, turn.

Row 10: 4 dc in first dc; * BPdc around next FPdc; sk next dc, dc in next 5 dc, sk next dc, BPdc around next FPdc; in next ch-1 sp work (4 dc, ch 1, 4 dc); rep from * across to turning ch; 5 dc in 3rd ch of turning ch-3; ch 3, turn.

Row 11: Dc in next 6 dc; * sk next dc, in next dc work (dc, ch 1, dc); sk next dc, dc in next 6 dc, in next ch-1 sp, and in next 6 dc; rep from * across to turning ch; dc in 3rd ch of turning ch-3; ch 3, turn.

Row 12: Dc in next 5 dc; * sk next dc, BPdc around next dc; in next ch-1 sp work (dc, ch 1, dc); BPdc around next dc; sk next dc, dc in next 11 dc; rep from * across to last 6 dc; sk next dc, dc in next 5 dc and in 3rd ch of turning ch-3; ch 3, turn.

Rep Rows 3 through 12 for pattern.

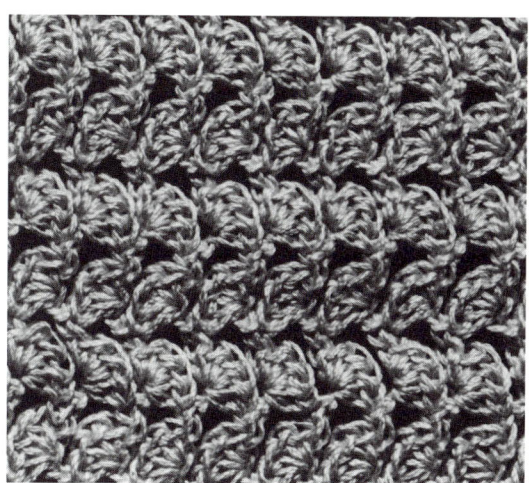

#41

Ch 2.

Row 1 (right side): 5 hdc in 2nd ch from hook; * ch 3, 5 hdc in 2nd ch from hook; rep from * to desired length; ch 5, turn.

Row 2: 5 hdc in 2nd ch from hook; sk next 4 hdc, sc in next hdc; * ch 3, 5 hdc in 2nd ch from hook; sk next 4 hdc, sc in next hdc; rep from * across; ch 5, turn.

Rep Row 2 for pattern.

10 + 2 chs

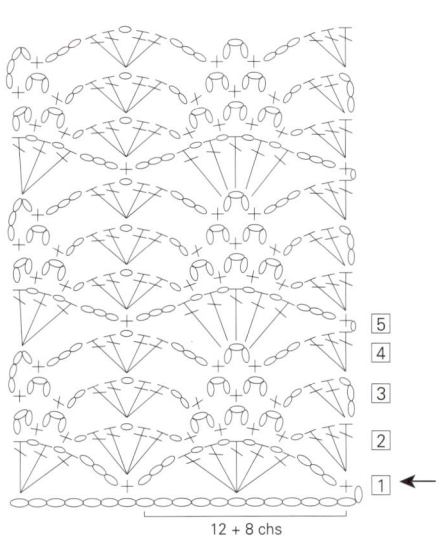
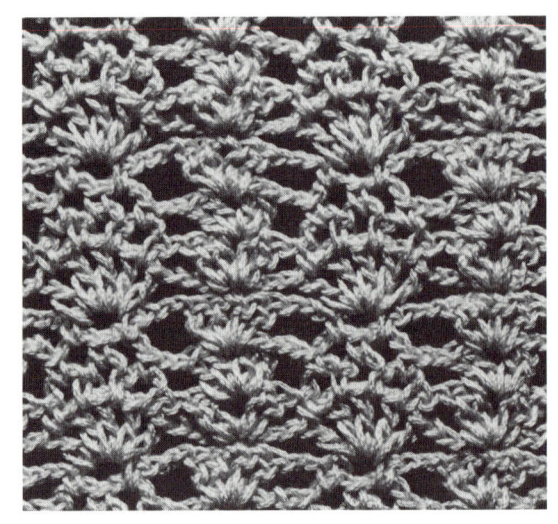

12 + 8 chs

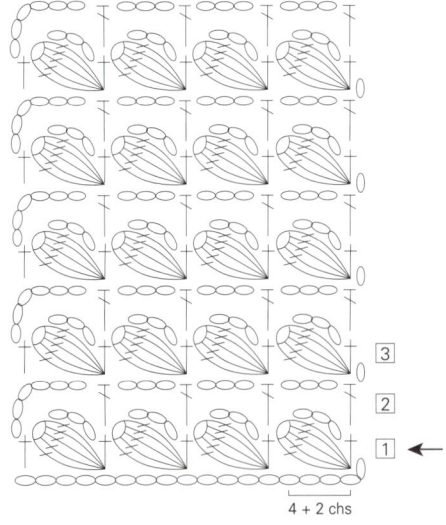
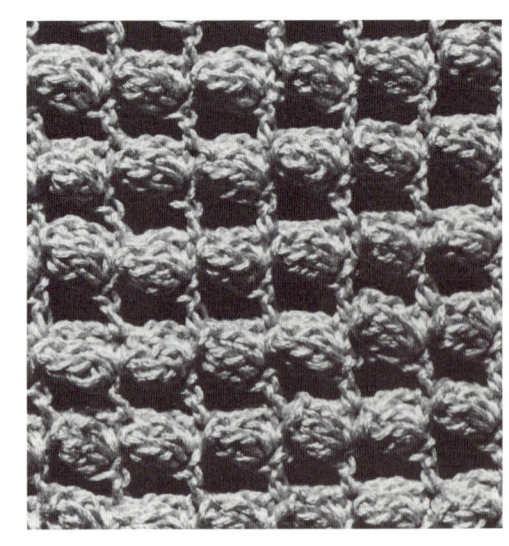

4 + 2 chs

#42

Multiple of 10 + 2

Row 1 (right side): Sc in 2nd and 3rd chs from hook; * ch 5, sk next 3 chs, sc in next ch, ch 5, sk next 3 chs, sc in next 3 chs; rep from * across to last 5 chs; sk next 3 chs, sc in last 2 chs; ch 5, turn.

Row 2: * (Sc in next ch-5 lp, ch 5) twice; sk next sc, sc in next sc, ch 5; rep from * across to last 2 ch-5 lps; sc in next ch-5 lp, ch 5, sc in last ch-5 lp, ch 2, sk next sc, dc in last sc; ch 1, turn.

Row 3: Sc in next dc; * ch 2, 7 dc in next ch-5 lp; ch 2, sc in next ch-5 lp, ch 5, sc in next ch-5 lp; rep from * across to turning ch; ch 2, sc in 3rd ch of turning ch-5; ch 3, turn.

Row 4: * (Dc in next dc, ch 1) 6 times; dc in next dc, sc in next ch-5 lp; rep from * across to last sc; dc in last sc; ch 5, turn.

Row 5: Sk next ch-1 sp; * 2 sc in each of next 4 ch-1 sps; ch 5, sk next 2 ch-1 sps; rep from * across to turning ch; ch 2, dc in 3rd ch of turning ch-3; ch 1, turn.

Row 6: Sc in next dc and in next ch-2 sp; * ch 5, sk next 3 sc, sc between next 2 sc, ch 5, 3 sc in next ch-5 lp; rep from * across to turning ch lp; ch 5, sc in lp and in 3rd ch of turning ch-5; ch 5, turn.

Rep Rows 2 through 6 for pattern.

#43

Multiple of 12 + 8

Row 1 (right side): Sc in 2nd ch from hook; * ch 3, sk next 5 chs, in next ch work (dc, ch 1) 4 times; dc in same ch; ch 3, sk next 5 chs, sc in next ch; rep from * across to last 6 chs; ch 3, sk next 5 chs, in last ch work (dc, ch 1, dc, ch 1, dc); ch 3, turn.

Row 2: Sc in next ch-1 sp, ch 3, sc in next ch-1 sp; * ch 1, in next sc work (2 dc, ch 1, 2 dc): shell made; ch 1, sc in next ch-1 sp, (ch 3, sc in next ch-1 sp) 3 times; rep from * across to last sc; ch 1, 3 dc in last sc; ch 3, turn.

Row 3: 2 dc in first dc; ch 2; * sc in next ch-3 lp, (ch 3, sc in next ch-3 lp) twice; ch 2, shell in ch-1 sp of next shell: shell in shell made; ch 2; rep from * across to last ch-3 lp; sc in last ch-3 lp, ch 3, sc in turning ch lp; ch 4, turn.

Row 4: Sc in next ch-3 lp, ch 3; * shell in next shell; ch 3, (sc in next ch-3 lp, ch 3) twice; rep from * across to turning ch; 3 dc in 3rd ch of turning ch-3; ch 1, turn.

Row 5: Sc in next dc, ch 3; * sk next ch-3 lp, in next ch-3 lp work (dc, ch 1) 4 times; dc in same lp; ch 3, sc in ch-1 sp of next shell; ch 3; rep from * across to turning ch lp, in lp work (dc, ch 1, dc, ch 1, dc); ch 3, turn.

Rep Rows 2 through 5 for pattern.

#44

Multiple of 4 + 2

> **PATTERN STITCH**
>
> **Popcorn** (PC): 5 dc in st, drop lp from hook, insert hook in first dc, draw dropped lp through, ch 1: PC made.

Row 1 (right side): Sc in 2nd ch from hook; * ch 3, PC (see Pattern Stitch) in same ch; (sk next 3 chs, sc in next ch; rep from * across; ch 6, turn.

Row 2: Sk first sc, dc in next sc; * ch 3, dc in next sc; rep from * across; ch 1, turn.

Row 3: In each dc work (sc, ch 3, PC); sc in 3rd ch of turning ch-6; ch 6, turn.

Rep Rows 2 and 3 for pattern.

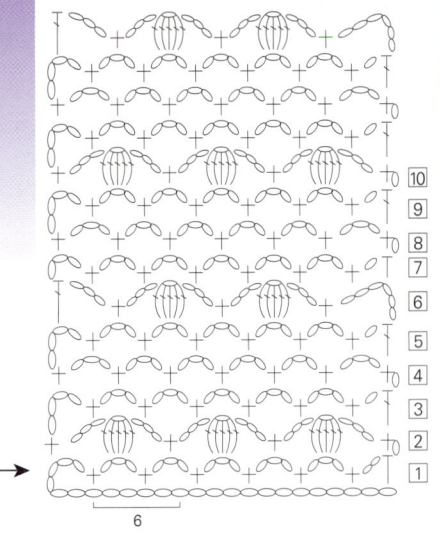

#45

Multiple of 6

> **PATTERN STITCH**
>
> **Popcorn** (PC): 5 dc in next lp, drop lp from hook, insert hook in first dc, draw dropped lp through, ch 1: PC made.

Row 1: Sc in 7th ch from hook; * ch 3, sk next 2 chs, sc in next ch; rep from * across to last 2 chs; ch 2, sk next ch, hdc in last ch; ch 1, turn.

Row 2 (right side): Sc in next hdc, ch 3, PC (see Pattern Stitch) in next ch-3 lp; * ch 3, sc in next ch-3 lp, ch 3, PC in next ch-3 lp; rep from * across to beg 6 skipped chs; ch 3, sc in 4th ch of 6 skipped chs; ch 4, turn.

Row 3: * Sc in next ch-3 lp, ch 3; rep from * across to last ch-3 lp; sc in last ch-3 lp, ch 1, dc in last sc; ch 1, turn.

Row 4: Sc in next dc; * ch 3, sc in next ch-3 lp; rep from * across to turning ch; sc in 3rd ch of turning ch-4; ch 4, turn.

Row 5: * Sc in next ch-3 lp, ch 3; rep from * across to last ch-3 lp; sc in last ch-3 lp, ch 1, dc in last sc; ch 6, turn.

Row 6: Sc in next ch-3 lp, ch 3; * PC in next ch-3 lp; ch 3, sc in next ch-3 lp, ch 3; rep from * across to turning ch; dc in 3rd ch of turning ch-4; ch 3, turn.

Row 7: * Sc in next ch-3 lp, ch 3; rep from * across to turning ch lp; sc in lp, ch 1, hdc in 3rd ch of turning ch-6; ch 1, turn.

Row 8: Sc in next hdc; * ch 3, sc in next ch-3 lp; rep from * across to turning ch; sc in 2nd ch of turning ch-3; ch 4, turn.

Row 9: * Sc in next ch-3 lp, ch 3; rep from * across to last ch-3 lp; sc in last ch-3 lp, ch 1, dc in last sc; ch 1, turn.

Row 10: Sc in next dc, ch 3, PC in next ch-3 lp; * ch 3, sc in next ch-3 lp, ch 3, PC in next ch-3 lp; rep from * across to turning ch; sc in 3rd ch of turning ch-4; ch 4, turn.

Rep Rows 3 through 10 for pattern.

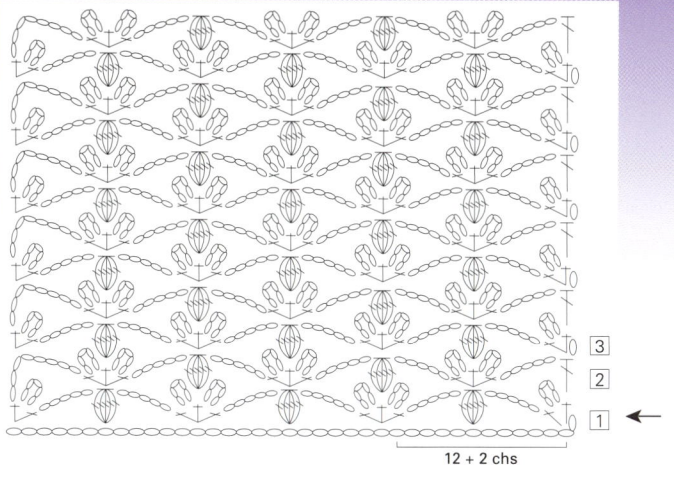
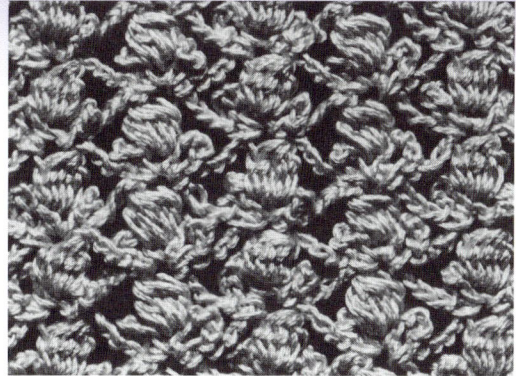

#46

Multiple of 12 + 2

> **PATTERN STITCH**
>
> **Cluster** (CL): Keeping last lp of each dc on hook, 5 dc in next st, YO and draw through all 6 lps on hook: CL made.

Row 1 (right side): In 2nd ch from hook work (sc, ch 5, sc); * ch 5, sk next 5 chs, CL (see Pattern Stitch) in next ch; ch 5, sk next 5 chs, in next ch work (sc, ch 5, sc, ch 5, sc); rep from * across to last ch; in last ch work (sc, ch 5, sc); ch 8, turn.

Row 2: * In next CL work (sc, ch 5, sc, ch 5, sc); ch 5, sk next ch-5 lp, CL in next sc; ch 5; rep from * to last sc; dc in last sc; ch 1, turn.

Row 3: In next dc work (sc, ch 5, sc); * ch 5, sk next ch-5 lp, CL in next sc; ch 5, in next CL work (sc, ch 5, sc, ch 5, sc); rep from * across to turning ch; in 3rd ch of turning ch-8 work (sc, ch 5, sc); ch 8, turn.

Rep Rows 2 and 3 for pattern.

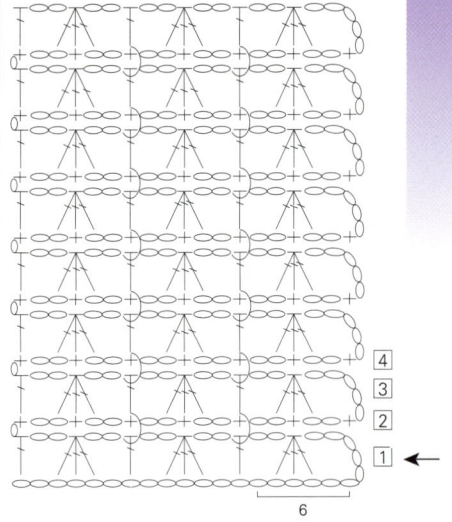
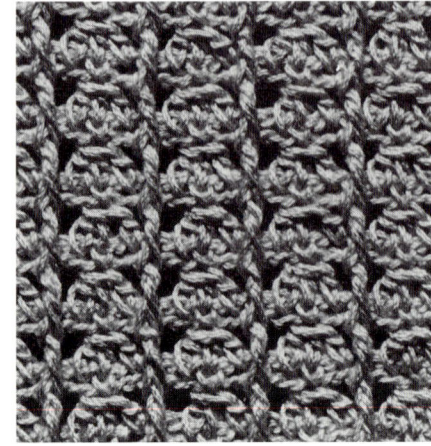

#47

Multiple of 6

> **PATTERN STITCHES**
>
> **Cluster** (CL): Keeping last lp of each dc on hook, dc in next 3 sts, YO and draw through all 4 lps on hook: CL made.
>
> **Front Post Double Crochet** (FPdc): YO, insert hook from front to back to front around post (see page 8) of next dc; YO and draw lp through, (YO and draw through 2 lps on hook) twice: FPdc made.

Row 1 (right side): CL (see Pattern Stitches) over 8th, 9th, and 10th chs from hook; ch 2, sk next ch, dc in next ch; * ch 2, sk next ch, CL over next 3 chs; ch 2, sk next ch, dc in next ch; rep from * across; ch 1, turn.

Row 2: Sc in next dc; * ch 2, sc in next CL, ch 2, sc in next dc; rep from * across to last CL; sc in last CL, ch 2, sc in 5th ch of beg 7 skipped chs; ch 5, turn.

Row 3: Sk next ch, CL over next ch, next sc, and next ch; * ch 2, sk next ch, FPdc (see Pattern Stitches) around dc in 2nd row below; ch 2, sk next ch, CL over next ch, next sc, and next ch; rep from * across to last sc; ch 2, dc in last sc; ch 1, turn.

Row 4: Sc in next dc; * ch 2, sc in next CL, ch 2, sc in next FPdc; rep from * across to last CL; sc in last CL, ch 2, sc in 3rd ch of turning ch-5; ch 5, turn.

Rep Rows 3 and 4 for pattern.

10 + 2 chs

#48

Multiple of 10 + 2

Row 1: Sc in 2nd ch from hook, ch 2, sk next ch; * sc in next ch, (ch 3, sk next 2 chs, sc in next ch) twice; ch 3, sk next 3 chs; rep from * across to last 2 chs; ch 2, sk next ch, sc in last ch; ch 4, turn.

Row 2 (right side): 4 trc in next ch-2 sp; * sc in next ch-3 lp, ch 3, sc in next ch-3 lp, 9 trc in next ch-3 lp; rep from * across to last ch-2 sp; 4 trc in last ch-2 sp; trc in last sc; ch 1, turn.

Row 3: Sc in next 2 trc; * ch 4, in next ch-3 lp work (sc, ch 3, sc); ch 4, sk next 3 trc, sc in next 3 trc; rep from * across to turning ch; sc in 4th ch of turning ch-4; ch 1, turn.

Row 4: * Sc in next sc, ch 3, sk next ch, sc in next ch, ch 3, sk next ch-3 lp and next 2 chs of next ch-4 lp, sc in next ch, ch 3, sk next sc; rep from * across to last sc; sc in last sc; ch 4, turn.

Row 5: * Sc in next ch-3 lp, 9 trc in next ch-3 lp; sc in next ch-3 lp, ch 3; rep from * across to last ch-3 lp; sc in last ch-3 lp, ch 1, dc in last sc; ch 1, turn.

Row 6: Sc in next dc and in next ch-1 sp; * ch 4, sk next 3 trc, sc in next 3 trc, ch 4, in next ch-3 lp work (sc, ch 3, sc); rep from * across to turning ch lp; sc in lp, sc in 3rd ch of turning ch-4; ch 5, turn.

Row 7: Sk next 2 chs of next ch-4 lp; * sc in next ch, ch 3, sk next sc, sc in next sc, ch 3, sk next ch of next ch-4 lp, sc in next ch, ch 3, sk next ch-3 lp and next 2 chs of next ch-4 lp; rep from * across to last sc; ch 2, dc in last sc; ch 4, turn.

Row 8: 4 trc in next ch-2 sp; * sc in next ch-3 lp, ch 3, sc in next ch-3 lp, 9 trc in next ch-3 lp; rep from * across to turning ch lp; 4 trc in lp; trc in 3rd ch of turning ch-5; ch 1, turn.

Rep Rows 3 through 8 for pattern.

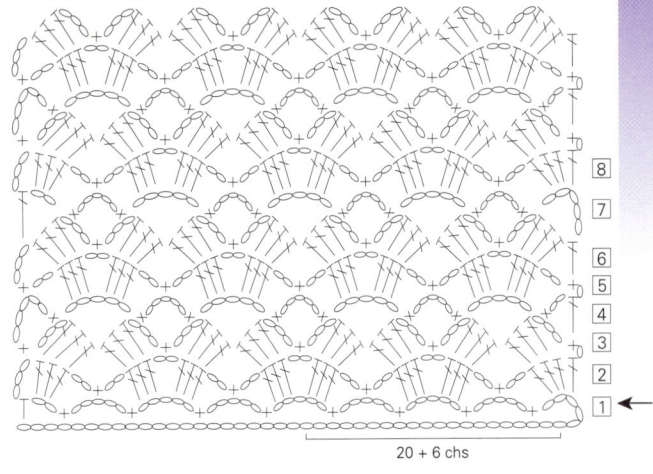

#49

Multiple of 20 + 6

Row 1 (right side): Sc in 8th ch from hook; * ch 5, sk next 4 chs, sc in next ch; rep from * across to last 3 chs; ch 2, sk next 2 chs, hdc in last ch; ch 3, turn.

Row 2: 3 dc in next ch-2 sp; * ch 2, sc in next ch-5 lp, ch 2, in next ch-5 lp work (3 dc, ch 2, 3 dc); rep from * across to lp formed by beg 7 skipped chs; 3 dc in lp; dc in 5th ch of 7 skipped chs; ch 1, turn.

Row 3: Sc in next dc, ch 3, dc in next 3 dc; * sk next sc, dc in next 3 dc, ch 3, sc in next ch-2 sp, ch 3, dc in next 3 dc; rep from * across to last 3 dc, dc in last 3 dc, ch 3, sc in 3rd ch of turning ch-3; ch 5, turn.

Row 4: * Sc in next ch-3 lp, ch 5; rep from * across to last ch-3 lp; sc in last ch-3 lp, ch 2, dc in last sc; ch 1, turn.

Row 5: Sc in next dc; * ch 2, in next ch-5 lp work (3 dc, ch 2, 3 dc); ch 2, sc in next ch-5 lp; rep from * across to turning ch; sc in 3rd ch of turning ch-5; ch 3, turn.

Row 6: * Dc in next 3 dc, ch 3, sc in next ch-2 sp, ch 3, dc in next 3 dc, sk next sc; rep from * across to last sc; dc in last sc; ch 5, turn.

Row 7: * Sc in next ch-3 lp, ch 5; rep from * across to turning ch; ch 2, dc in 3rd ch of turning ch-3; ch 3, turn.

Row 8: 3 dc in next ch-2 sp; * ch 2, sc in next ch-5 lp, ch 2, in next ch-5 lp work (3 dc, ch 2, 3 dc); rep from * across to turning ch lp; 3 dc in lp; dc in 3rd ch of turning ch-5; ch 1, turn.

Rep Rows 3 through 8 for pattern.

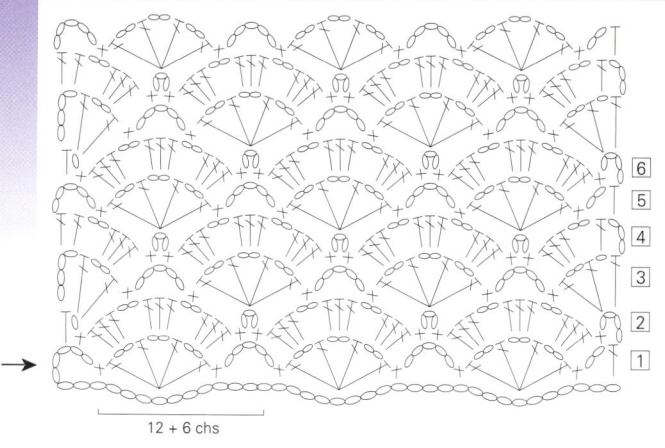

#50

Multiple of 12 + 6

Row 1: Sc in 8th ch from hook; * sk next 3 chs, in next ch work (dc, ch 2) 3 times; dc in same ch; sk next 3 chs, sc in next ch, ch 5, sk next 3 chs, sc in next ch; rep from * across to last 2 chs; ch 2, sk next ch, dc in last ch; ch 4, turn.

Row 2 (right side): Sc in next ch-2 sp; * (3 dc in next ch-2 sp, ch 2) twice; 3 dc in next ch-2 sp; in next ch-5 lp work (sc, ch 3, sc); rep from * across to lp formed by beg 7 skipped chs; sc in lp, ch 1, hdc in 5th ch of 7 skipped chs; ch 4, turn.

Row 3: In next ch-1 sp work (dc, ch 2, dc); * sc in next ch-2 sp, ch 5, sc in next ch-2 sp, in next ch-3 lp work (dc, ch 2) 3 times; dc in same lp; rep from * across to turning ch lp; in turning ch lp work (dc, ch 2, dc); ch 1, dc in 3rd ch of turning ch-4; ch 3, turn.

Row 4: Dc in next ch-1 sp, ch 2; * 3 dc in next ch-2 sp; in next ch-5 lp work (sc, ch 3, sc); (3 dc in next ch-2 sp, ch 2) twice; rep from * across to turning ch lp; dc in turning ch lp and in 3rd ch of turning ch-4; ch 5, turn.

Row 5: Sc in next ch-2 sp; * in next ch-3 lp work (dc, ch 2) 3 times; dc in same lp; sc in next ch-2 sp, ch 5, sc in next ch-2 sp; rep from * across to turning ch; ch 2, hdc in 3rd ch of turning ch-3; ch 4, turn.

Row 6: Sc in next ch-2 sp; * (3 dc in next ch-2 sp, ch 2) twice; 3 dc in next ch-2 sp; in next ch-5 lp work (sc, ch 3, sc); rep from * across to turning ch lp; sc in lp, ch 1, hdc in 3rd ch of turning ch-5; ch 4, turn.

Rep Rows 3 through 6 for pattern.

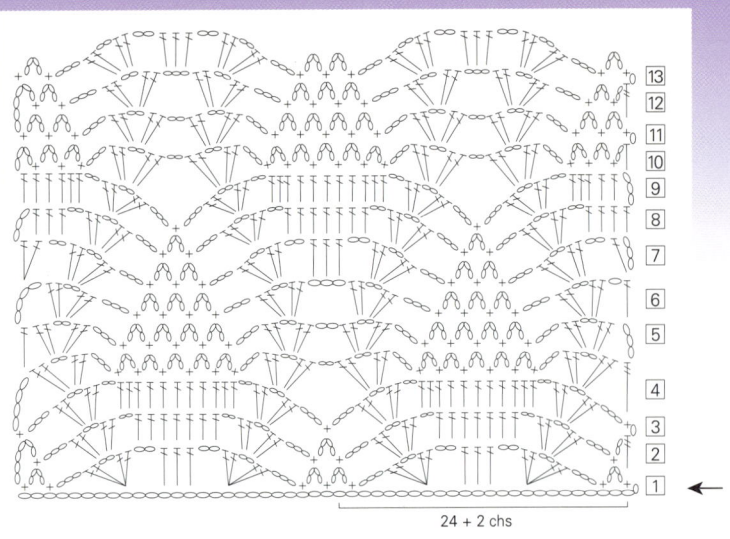

#51

Multiple of 24 + 2

Row 1 (right side): Sc in 2nd ch from hook, ch 4, sk next ch, sc in next ch; * ch 3, sk next 5 chs, in next ch work (2 dc, ch 2, 2 dc); ch 2, sk next 2 chs, dc in next 3 chs, ch 2, sk next 2 chs, in next ch work (2 dc, ch 2, 2 dc); ch 3, sk next 5 chs, (sc in next ch, ch 4, sk next ch) twice; sc in next ch; rep from * across to last 2 chs; ch 4, sk next ch, sc in last ch; ch 6, turn.

Row 2: * Sc in next ch-4 lp, ch 3, in next ch-2 sp work (2 dc, ch 2, 2 dc); ch 2, 2 dc in next ch-2 sp; dc in next 3 dc, 2 dc in next ch-2 sp; ch 2, in next ch-2 sp work (2 dc, ch 2, 2 dc); ch 3, sc in next ch-4 lp, ch 4; rep from * across to last ch-4 lp; sc in last ch-4 lp, ch 2, trc in last sc; ch 1, turn.

Row 3: Sc in next trc; * ch 3, in next ch-2 sp work (2 dc, ch 2, 2 dc); ch 2, 2 dc in next ch-2 sp; dc in next 7 dc, 2 dc in next ch-2 sp; ch 2, in next ch-2 sp work (2 dc, ch 2, 2 dc); ch 3, sc in next ch-4 lp; rep from * across to turning ch; sc in 4th ch of turning ch-6; ch 4, turn.

Row 4: Sk next ch-3 lp; * in next ch-2 sp work (2 dc, ch 2, 2 dc); ch 3, sk next ch-2 sp, (sc in next dc, ch 4, sk next dc) 5 times; sc in next dc, ch 3, sk next ch-2 sp, in next ch-2 sp work (2 dc, ch 2, 2 dc); ch 2; rep from * across to last ch-2 sp; in last ch-2 sp work (2 dc, ch 2, 2 dc); trc in last sc; ch 3, turn.

Row 5: * In next ch-2 sp work (2 dc, ch 2, 2 dc); ch 3, sk next ch-3 lp, (sc in next ch-4 lp, ch 4) 4 times; sc in next ch-4 lp, ch 3, in next ch-2 sp work (2 dc, ch 2, 2 dc); ch 2, sk next ch-2 sp; rep from * across to last ch-2 sp; in last ch-2 sp work (2 dc, ch 2, 2 dc); dc in 4th ch of turning ch-4; ch 4, turn.

Row 6: * In next ch-2 sp work (2 dc, ch 2, 2 dc); ch 3, sk next ch-3 lp, (sc in next ch-4 lp, ch 4) 3 times; sc in next ch-4 lp, ch 3, sk next ch-3 lp, in next ch-2 sp work (2 dc, ch 2, 2 dc); ch 3, sk next ch-2 sp; rep from * across to last ch-2 sp; in last ch-2 sp work (2 dc, ch 2, 2 dc); ch 1, dc in 3rd ch of turning ch-3; ch 3, turn.

Row 7: Dc in first dc; * ch 2, in next ch-2 sp work (2 dc, ch 2, 2 dc); ch 3, sk next ch-3 lp, (sc in next ch-4 lp, ch 4) twice; sc in next ch-4 lp, ch 3, sk next ch-3 lp, in next ch-2 sp work (2 dc, ch 2, 2 dc); ch 2, 3 dc in next ch-3 lp; rep from * across to turning ch-4; 2 dc in 3rd ch of turning ch-4; ch 3 (counts as first dc on following rows), turn.

Row 8: Dc in next dc; * 2 dc in next ch-2 sp; ch 2, in next ch-2 sp work (2 dc, ch 2, 2 dc); ch 3, sk next ch-3 lp, sc in next ch-4 lp, ch 4, sc in next ch-4 lp, ch 3, sk next ch-3 lp, in next ch-2 sp work (2 dc, ch 2, 2 dc); ch 2, 2 dc in next ch-2 sp; dc in next 3 dc; rep from * across to turning ch; dc in 3rd ch of turning ch-3; ch 3, turn.

Row 9: Dc in next 3 dc; * 2 dc in next ch-2 sp; ch 2, in next ch-2 sp work (2 dc, ch 2, 2 dc); ch 3, sk next ch-3 lp, sc in next ch-4 lp, ch 3, sk next ch-3 lp, in next ch-2 sp work (2 dc, ch 2, 2 dc); ch 2, 2 dc in next ch-2 sp; dc in next 7 dc; rep from * across to turning ch; dc in 3rd ch of turning ch-3; ch 4, turn.

Row 10: Sk first dc, (sc in next dc, ch 4, sk next dc) twice; * sc in next dc, ch 3, sk next ch-2 sp, in next ch-2 sp work (2 dc, ch 2, 2 dc); ch 2, in next ch-2 sp work (2 dc, ch 2, 2 dc); ch 3, sk next ch-2 sp, (sc in next dc, ch 4, sk next dc) 5 times; rep from * across to turning ch; ch 2, hdc in 3rd ch of turning ch-3; ch 1, turn.

Row 11: Sc in next hdc, (ch 4, sc in next ch-4 lp) twice; * ch 3, sk next ch-3 lp, in next ch-2 sp work (2 dc, ch 2, 2 dc); ch 2, sk next ch-2 sp, in next ch-2 sp work (2 dc, ch 2, 2 dc); ch 3, sk next ch-3 lp, (sc in next ch-4 lp, ch 4) 4 times; sc in next ch-4 lp; rep from * across to turning ch lp; sc in lp; ch 6, turn.

Row 12: Sc in next ch-4 lp, ch 4; * sc in next ch-4 lp, ch 3, sk next ch-3 lp, in next ch-2 sp work (2 dc, ch 2, 2 dc); ch 3, sk next ch-2 sp, in next ch-2 sp work (2 dc, ch 2, 2 dc); ch 3, sk next ch-3 lp, (sc in next ch-4 lp, ch 4) 3 times; rep from * across to last ch-4 lp; sc in last ch-4 lp, ch 2, trc in last sc; ch 1, turn.

Row 13: Sc in next trc, ch 4; * sc in next ch-4 lp, ch 3, sk next ch-3 lp, in next ch-2 sp work (2 dc, ch 2, 2 dc); ch 2, 3 dc in next ch-3 lp; ch 2, in next ch-2 sp work (2 dc, ch 2, 2 dc); ch 3, sk next ch-3 lp, (sc in next ch-4 lp, ch 4) twice; rep from * across to turning ch; sc in 4th ch of turning ch-6; ch 6, turn.

Rep Rows 2 through 13 for pattern.

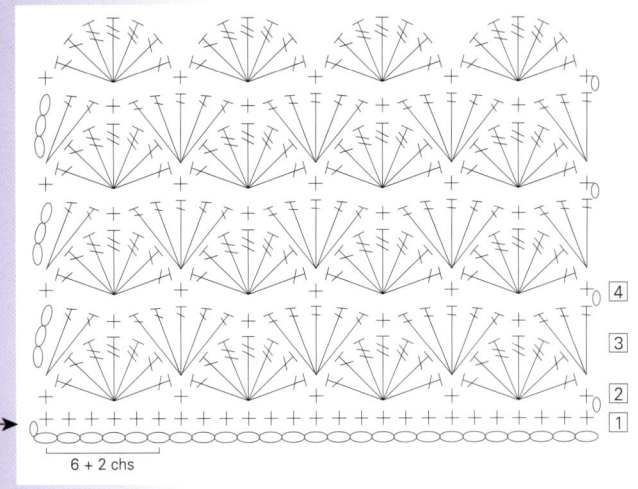

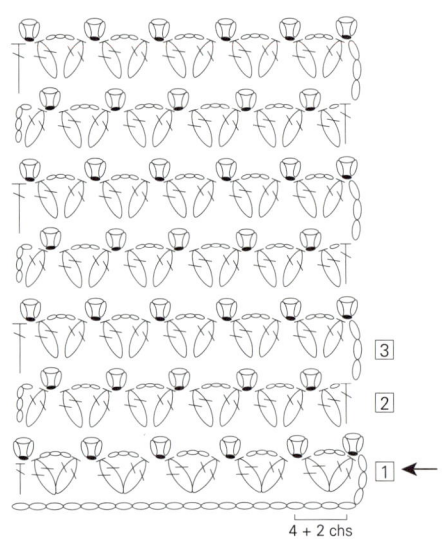

#52

Multiple of 6 + 2

Row 1: Sc in 2nd ch from hook and in each rem ch across; ch 1, turn.

Row 2 (right side): Sc in next sc; * sk next 2 sc, in next sc work (2 dc, 3 trc, 2 dc): shell made; sk next 2 sc, sc in next sc; rep from * across; ch 3, turn.

Row 3: 2 dc in first sc; * sk next 2 dc and next trc, sc in next trc, 5 dc in next sc; rep from * across to last 8 sts; sk next 2 dc and next trc, sc in next trc, 3 dc in next sc; ch 1, turn.

Row 4: Sc in next dc, shell in next sc; * sk next 2 dc, sc in next dc, sk next 2 dc, shell in next sc; rep from * across to last 2 dc; sk next 2 dc, sc in 3rd ch of turning ch-3; ch 3, turn.

Rep Rows 3 and 4 for pattern.

#53

Multiple of 4 + 2

PATTERN STITCH

Cluster (CL): Keeping last lp of each dc on hook, 2 dc in next st, YO and draw through all 3 lps on hook: CL made.

Row 1 (right side): Sl st in 4th ch from hook: picot made; * sk next 3 chs, in next ch work [CL (see Pattern Stitch), ch 3, CL]; ch 3, sl st in top of last CL made: ch-3 picot made; rep from * across to last 2 chs; sk next ch, dc in last ch; ch 4, turn.

Row 2: CL in next picot; ch-3 picot; * in next picot work (CL, ch 3, CL, ch-3 picot); rep from * across to last picot; in last picot work (CL, ch 1, dc); ch 6, turn.

Row 3: Sl st in 4th ch from hook: picot made; * in next picot work (CL, ch 3, CL, ch-3 picot); rep from * across to turning ch; dc in 3rd ch of turning ch-4; ch 4, turn.

Rep Rows 2 and 3 for pattern.

#54

Multiple of 8 + 1

Row 1 (right side): 3 dc in 5th ch from hook; sk next 3 chs, sc in next ch; * sk next 5 chs, 3 dc in next ch; ch 2, working over last 3 dc made, 3 dc in 2nd ch from last sc made; sk next ch, sc in next ch; rep from * across; ch 6, turn.

Row 2: Sc in next ch-2 sp; * ch 3, dc in next sc, ch 3, sc in next ch-2 sp; rep from * across to beg 4 skipped chs, sc in 3rd ch of 4 skipped chs; ch 1, turn.

Row 3: Sc in next sc; * sk next ch-3 lp, 3 dc in next ch-3 lp; ch 2, working over last 3 dc made, 3 dc in skipped ch-3 lp; sc in next sc; rep from * across to turning ch; in 3rd ch of turning ch-6 work (3 dc, ch 1, dc); ch 1, turn.

Row 4: Sc in next dc, ch 3, dc in next sc; * ch 3, sc in next ch-2 sp; ch 3, dc in next sc; rep from * across; ch 4, turn.

Row 5: 3 dc in first dc; sc in next sc; * sk next ch-3 lp, 3 dc in next ch-3 lp; ch 2, working over last 3 dc made, 3 dc in skipped lp; sc in next sc; rep from * across; ch 6, turn.

Row 6: Sc in next ch-2 sp; * ch 3, dc in next sc, ch 3, sc in next ch-2 sp; rep from * across to turning ch; sc in 3rd ch of turning ch-4; ch 1, turn.

Rep Rows 3 through 6 for pattern.

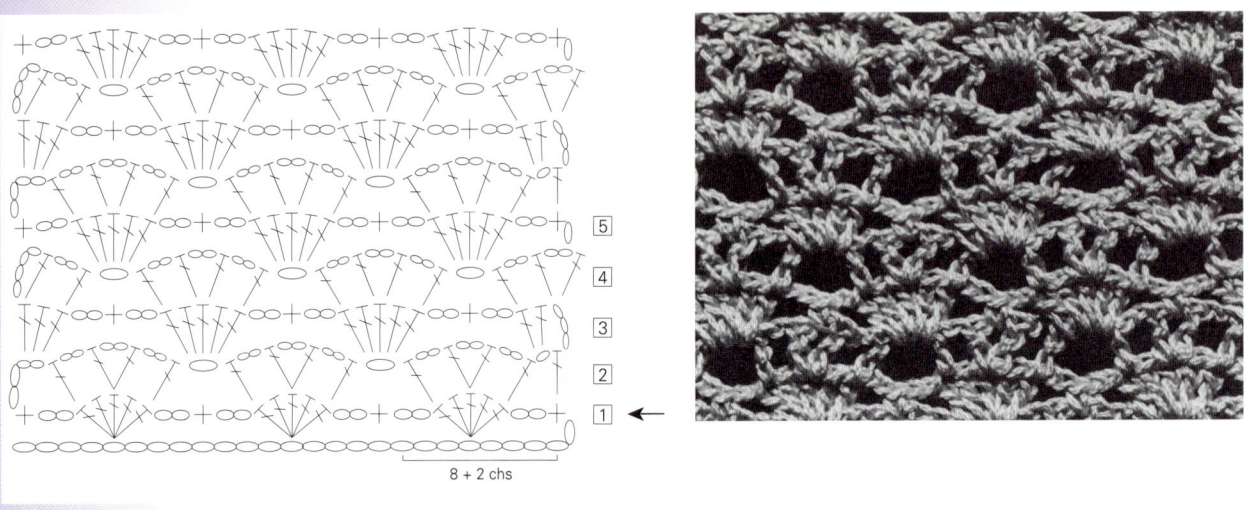

8 + 2 chs

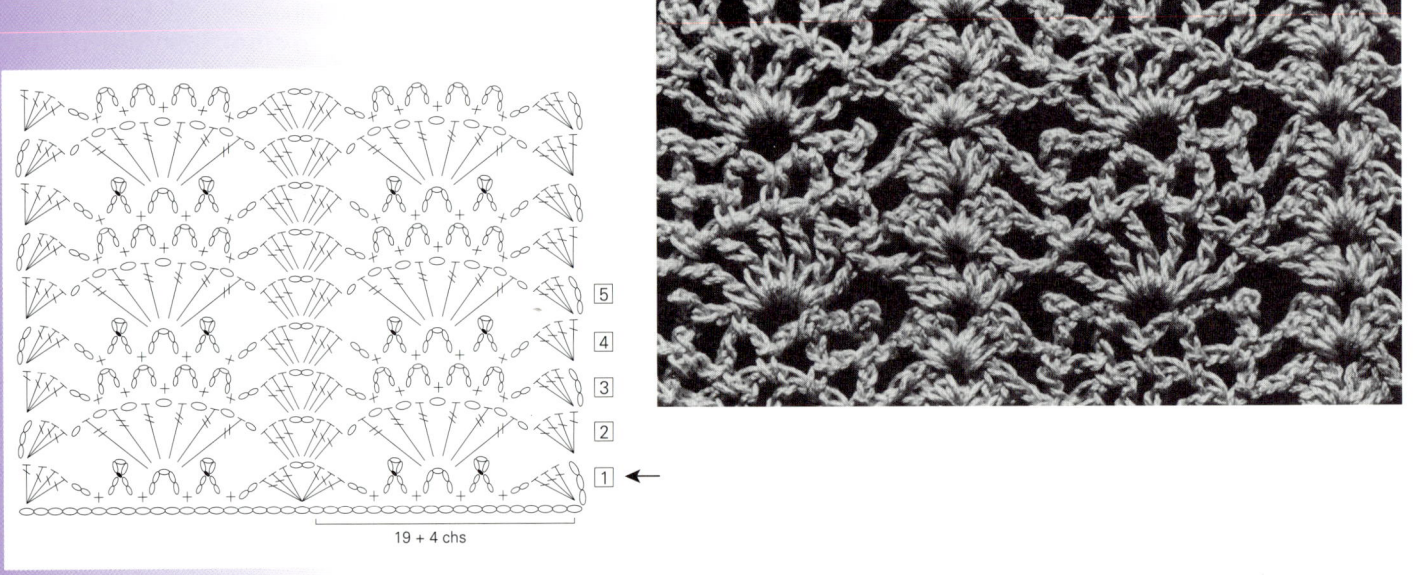

19 + 4 chs

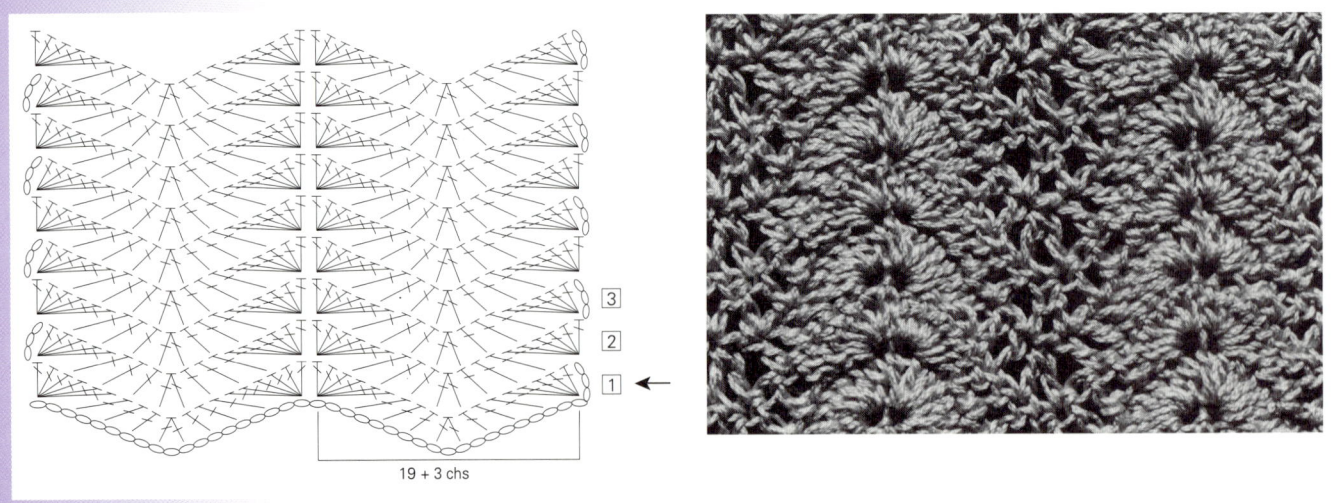

19 + 3 chs

#55

Multiple of 8 + 2

Row 1 (right side): Sc in 2nd ch from hook; * ch 2, sk next 3 chs, 5 dc in next ch; ch 2, sk next 3 chs, sc in next ch; rep from * across; ch 4, turn.

Row 2: Sk next sc; * dc in next dc, ch 2, sk next dc, in next dc work (dc, ch 2, dc); ch 2, sk next dc, dc in next dc, ch 1, sk next sc; rep from * across to last sc; dc in last sc; ch 3, turn.

Row 3: 2 dc in next ch-1 sp; * ch 2, sk next ch-2 sp, sc in next ch-2 sp, ch 2, sk next ch-2 sp, 5 dc in next ch-1 sp; rep from * across to turning ch lp; 2 dc in lp; dc in 3rd ch of turning ch-4; ch 4, turn.

Row 4: Dc in first dc; * ch 2, sk next dc, dc in next dc, ch 1, dc in next dc, ch 2, sk next dc, in next dc work (dc, ch 2, dc); rep from * across to turning ch; in 3rd ch of turning ch-3 work (dc, ch 2, dc); ch 1, turn.

Row 5: * Sc in next ch-2 sp, ch 2, sk next ch-2 sp, 5 dc in next ch-1 sp; ch 2, sk next ch-2 sp; rep from * across to turning ch; sc in 3rd ch of turning ch-4; ch 4, turn.

Rep Rows 2 through 5 for pattern.

#56

Multiple of 19 + 4

Row 1 (right side): 3 dc in 4th ch from hook; * ch 2, sk next 4 chs, sc in next ch, ch 5, sl st in 3rd ch from hook: picot made; ch 2, sk next 2 chs, sc in next ch, ch 5, sk next 2 chs, sc in next ch, ch 5, sl st in 3rd ch from hook: picot made; ch 2, sk next 2 chs, sc in next ch, ch 2, sk next 4 chs, in next ch work (3 dc, ch 2, 3 dc); rep from * across to last 5 chs; ch 2, sk next 4 chs, 4 dc in last ch; ch 3, turn.

Row 2: 3 dc in first dc; * ch 1, sk next picot, in next ch-5 lp work (trc, ch 1) 6 times; sk next picot, next sc, and next 3 dc; in next ch-2 sp work (3 dc, ch 2, 3 dc); rep from * across to last 3 dc; sk last 3 dc, 4 dc in 3rd ch of beg 3 skipped chs; ch 3, turn.

Row 3: 3 dc in first dc; * ch 2, sk next ch-1 sp, (sc in next ch-1 sp, ch 5) 4 times; sc in next ch-1 sp, ch 2, in next ch-2 sp work (3 dc, ch 2, 3 dc); rep from * across to last 3 dc; sk last 3 dc; 4 dc in 3rd ch of turning ch-3; ch 3, turn.

Row 4: 3 dc in first dc; * ch 2, sc in next ch-5 lp, ch 5, picot, ch 2, sc in next ch-5 lp, ch 5, sc in next ch-5 lp; ch 5, picot, ch 2, sc in next ch-5 lp, ch 2, sk next ch-2 sp, in next ch-2 sp work (3 dc, ch 2, 3 dc); rep from * across to last 3 dc; sk last 3 dc, 4 dc in 3rd ch of turning ch-3; ch 3, turn.

Row 5: 3 dc in first dc; * ch 1, sk next picot, in next ch-5 lp work (trc, ch 1) 6 times; sk next picot, next sc, and next 3 dc; in next ch-2 sp work (3 dc, ch 2, 3 dc); rep from * across to last 3 dc; sk last 3 dc, 4 dc in 3rd ch of turning ch-3; ch 3, turn.

Rep Rows 3 through 5 for pattern.

#57

Multiple of 19 + 3

Row 1 (right side): 5 dc in 4th ch from hook; (sk next ch, dc in next ch) 3 times; sk next ch, dec over next 3 chs (to work dec: keeping last lp of each dc on hook, dc in next ch, sk next ch, dc in next ch, YO and draw through all 3 lps on hook: dec made); (sk next ch, dc in next ch) 3 times; sk next ch; * 6 dc in each of next 2 chs; (sk next ch, dc in next ch) 3 times; sk next ch, dec as before; sk next ch, (dc in next ch, sk next ch) 3 times; rep from * across to last ch; 6 dc in last ch; ch 3, turn.

Row 2: 5 dc in first dc; (sk next dc, dc in next dc) 3 times; sk next dc, dec over next 3 sts; sk next dc, (dc in next dc, sk next dc) 3 times; * 6 dc in each of next 2 dc; sk next dc, (dc in next dc, sk next dc) 3 times; dec over next 3 sts; sk next dc, (dc in next dc, sk next dc) 3 times; rep from * across to beg 3 skipped chs; 6 dc in 3rd ch of 3 skipped chs; ch 3, turn.

Row 3: 5 dc in first dc; (sk next dc, dc in next dc) 3 times; sk next dc, dec over next 3 sts; sk next dc, (dc in next dc, sk next dc) 3 times; * 6 dc in each of next 2 dc; sk next dc, (dc in next dc, sk next dc) 3 times; dec over next 3 sts; sk next dc, (dc in next dc, sk next dc) 3 times; rep from * across to turning ch; 6 dc in 3rd ch of turning ch-3; ch 3, turn.

Rep Row 3 for pattern.

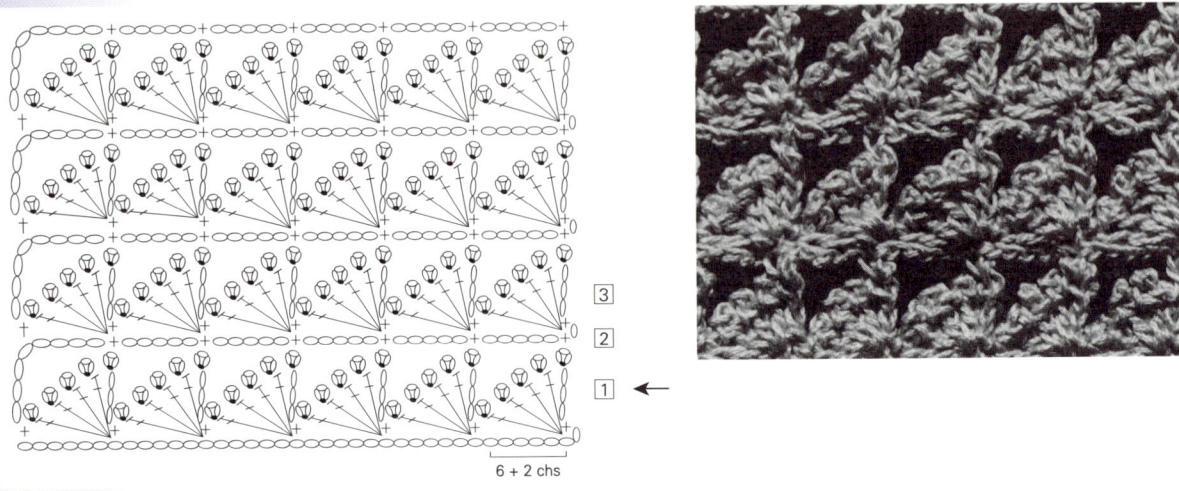

6 + 2 chs

18 + 2 chs

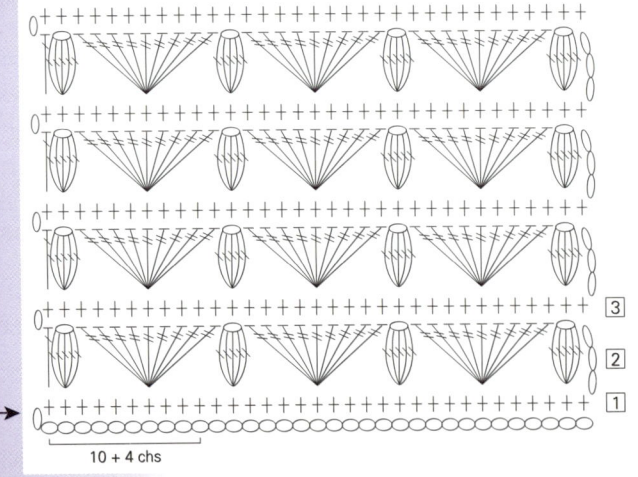

10 + 4 chs

#58

Multiple of 6 + 2

Row 1 (right side): Sc in 2nd ch from hook; * ch 6, sl st in 3rd ch from hook: picot made; in same ch work (dc, ch 3, sl st in dc just made: ch-3 picot made) 4 times; sk next 5 chs, sc in next ch; rep from * across; ch 8, turn.

Row 2: * Sk next 4 picots, sc in next picot, ch 5; rep from * across to last picot, sc in last picot; ch 1, turn.

Row 3: Sc in next sc; * ch 6, sl st in 3rd ch from hook: picot made; in same sc work (dc, ch-3 picot) 4 times; sc in next sc; rep from * across to turning ch; sc in 4th ch of turning ch-8; ch 8, turn.

Rep Rows 2 and 3 for pattern.

#59

Multiple of 18 + 2

Row 1: Sc in 2nd ch from hook; * ch 2, sk next 2 chs, sc in next ch, (ch 3, sk next 3 chs, sc in next ch) 3 times; ch 2, sk next 2 chs, sc in next ch; rep from * across; ch 1, turn.

Row 2 (right side): In next sc work (sc, ch 3, dc); * sc in next ch-3 lp, 6 dc in next ch-3 lp; sc in next ch-3 lp, sk next sc, in next sc work (dc, ch 3, sc, ch 3, dc); rep from * across to last sc; in last sc work (dc, ch 3, sc); ch 5, turn.

Row 3: * Sc in next ch-3 lp, ch 1, sk next dc and next sc, (dc in next dc, ch 1) 6 times; sc in next ch-3 lp, ch 2, dc in next sc, ch 2; rep from * across to last sc; dc in last sc; ch 1, turn.

Row 4: * Sc in next dc, sk next sc, dc in next dc and in next ch-1 sp, (2 dc in next dc, dc in next ch-1 sp) 4 times; dc in next dc, sk next sc; rep from * across to turning ch; sc in 3rd ch of turning ch-5; ch 5, turn.

Row 5: * Sk next 2 dc, sc in next dc, ch 3, sk next 3 dc, sc in next dc, ch 3, sk next dc, sc in next dc, ch 3, sk next 3 dc, sc in next dc, ch 2, dc in next sc, ch 2; rep from * across to last sc; dc in last sc; ch 1, turn.

Row 6: In next dc work (sc, ch 3, dc); * sc in next ch-3 lp, 6 dc in next ch-3 lp; sc in next ch-3 lp, sk next sc, in next dc work (dc, ch 3, sc, ch 3, dc); rep from * across to turning ch; in 3rd ch of turning ch-5 work (dc, ch 3, sc); ch 5, turn.

Rep Rows 3 through 6 for pattern.

#60

Multiple of 10 + 4

> **PATTERN STITCH**
>
> **Popcorn** (PC): 5 dc in next sp, drop lp from hook, insert hook in first dc made, draw dropped lp through, ch 1: PC made.

Row 1: Sc in 2nd ch from hook and in each rem ch; ch 3 (counts as first dc on following rows), turn.

Row 2 (right side): PC (see Pattern Stitch) in next sc; * sk next 4 sc, 9 trc in next sc; sk next 4 sc, PC in next sc; rep from * across to last sc; dc in last sc; ch 1, turn.

Row 3: Sc in each st and in each PC across to turning ch; sc in 3rd ch of turning ch-3; ch 3, turn.

Rep Rows 2 and 3 for pattern.

#61

Multiple of 8 + 2

> **PATTERN STITCH**
>
> **Cluster** (CL): Keeping last lp of each dc on hook, 4 dc in next ch, YO and draw through all 5 lps on hook: CL made.

Row 1: Sc in 2nd ch from hook, ch 4, sk next 3 chs, CL (see Pattern Stitch) in next ch; ch 5, sk next 3 chs; * in next ch work (sc, ch 1, sc); ch 4, sk next 3 chs, CL in next ch; ch 5, sk next 3 chs; rep from * across to last ch; sc in last ch; ch 3, turn.

Row 2 (right side): 2 dc in first sc; ch 2, sc in next CL, ch 2; * 6 dc in next ch-1 sp; ch 2, sc in next CL, ch 2; rep from * across to last sc; 3 dc in last sc; ch 7, turn.

Row 3: In next sc work (sc, ch 1, sc); ch 4, sk next 2 dc; * CL between next 2 dc; ch 5, in next sc work (sc, ch 1, sc); ch 4, sk next 2 dc; rep from * across to turning ch; dc in 3rd ch of turning ch-3; ch 1, turn.

Row 4: Sc in next dc, ch 2, 6 dc in next ch-1 sp; * ch 2, sc in next CL, ch 2, 6 dc in next ch-1 sp; rep from * across to turning ch; ch 2, sc in 3rd ch of turning ch-7; ch 1, turn.

Row 5: Sc in next sc, ch 4, sk next 2 dc, CL between next 2 dc; ch 5; * in next sc work (sc, ch 1, sc); ch 4, sk next 2 dc, CL between next 2 dc; ch 5; rep from * across to last sc; sc in last sc; ch 3, turn.

Rep Rows 2 through 5 for pattern.

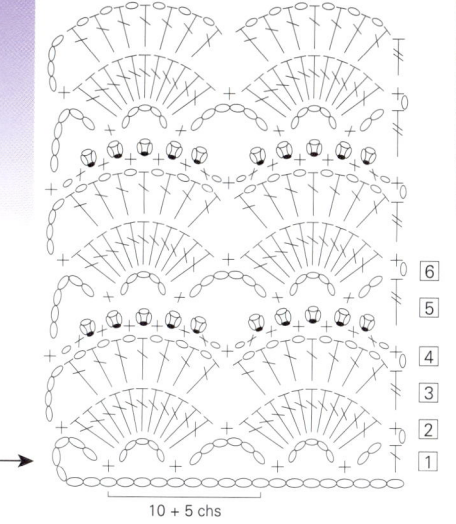

#62

Multiple of 10 + 5

Row 1: Sc in 8th ch from hook, ch 5, sk next 3 chs, sc in next ch; * ch 6, sk next 5 chs, sc in next ch, ch 5, sk next 3 chs, sc in next ch; rep from * across to last 3 chs; ch 2, sk next 2 chs, dc in last ch; ch 1, turn.

Row 2 (right side): Sc in next dc, 11 dc in next ch-5 lp; * sc in next ch-6 lp, 11 dc in next ch-5 lp; rep from * across to beg 7 skipped chs; sc in 5th ch of 7 skipped chs; ch 4, turn.

Row 3: Sk next 2 dc; * (dc in next dc, ch 1) 6 times; dc in next dc, sk next 2 dc, next sc, and next 2 dc; rep from * across to last 3 sts; sk next 2 dc, trc in last sc; ch 1, turn.

Row 4: Sc in next trc; * ch 1, (sc in next ch-1 sp, ch 3, sl st in 3rd ch from hook: picot made) 5 times; sc in next ch-1 sp, ch 1, sc between next 2 dc; rep from * across to turning ch; sc in 4th ch of turning ch-4; ch 6, turn.

Row 5: Sk next picot; * sc in next picot, ch 5, sk next picot, sc in next picot, ch 6, sk next 2 picots; rep from * across to last sc; ch 2, trc in last sc; ch 1, turn.

Row 6: Sc in next trc, 11 dc in next ch-5 lp; * sc in next ch-6 lp, 11 dc in next ch-5 lp; rep from * across to turning ch; sc in 4th ch of turning ch-6; ch 4, turn.

Rep Rows 3 through 6 for pattern.

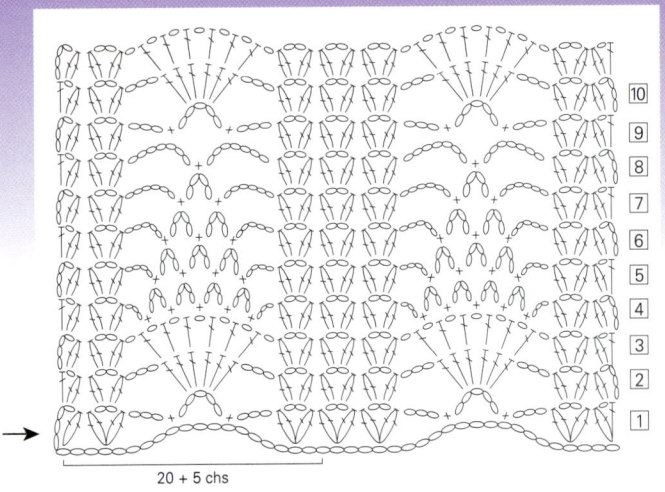

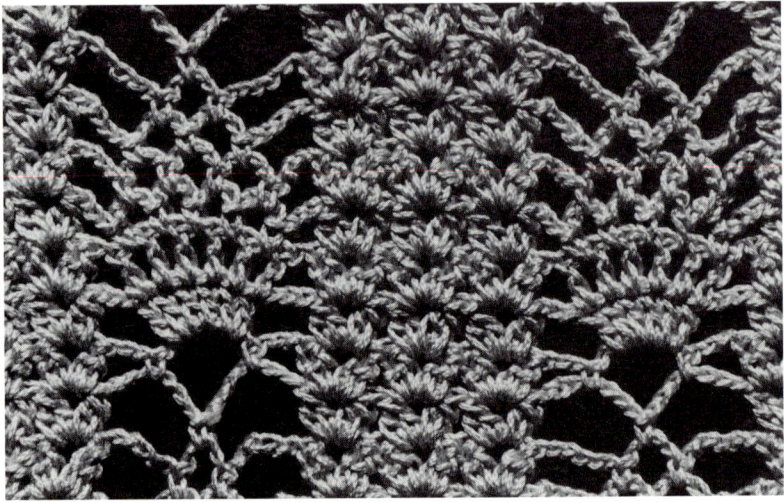

#63

Multiple of 20 + 5

PATTERN STITCH

Cluster (CL): Keeping last lp of each dc on hook, 2 dc in st, YO and draw through all 3 lps on hook: CL made.

Row 1: CL (see Pattern Stitches) in 5th ch from hook; sk next 2 chs, in next ch work (CL, ch 2, CL): shell made; * ch 3, sk next 4 chs, sc in next ch, ch 5, sk next 3 chs, sc in next ch, ch 3, sk next 4 chs, (shell in next ch, sk next 2 chs) twice; shell in next ch; rep from * across to last 3 chs; sk next 2 chs, in last ch work (CL, ch 1, dc); ch 4, turn.

Row 2 (right side): CL in next ch-1 sp; shell in ch-2 sp of next shell: shell in shell made; * ch 3, 6 dc in next ch-5 lp; ch 3, shell in each of next 3 shells; rep from * across to lp formed by beg 4 skipped chs; CL in lp; ch 1, dc in 3rd ch of 4 skipped chs; ch 4, turn.

Row 3: CL in next ch-1 sp; shell in next shell; * ch 1, (dc in next dc, ch 1) 6 times; shell in each of next 3 shells; rep from * across to turning ch lp; CL in lp; ch 1, dc in 3rd ch of turning ch-4; ch 4, turn.

Row 4: CL in next ch-1 sp; shell in next shell; * ch 3, sk next ch-1 sp, (sc in next ch-1 sp, ch 4) 4 times; sc in

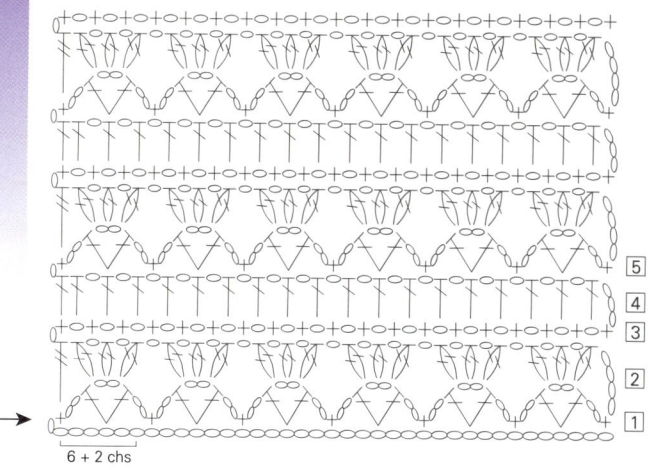

next ch-1 sp, ch 3, shell in each of next 3 shells; rep from * across to turning ch lp; CL in lp; ch 1, dc in 3rd ch of turning ch-4; ch 4, turn.

Row 5: CL in next ch-1 sp; shell in next shell; * ch 4, (sc in next ch-4 lp, ch 4) 4 times; shell in each of next 3 shells; rep from * across to turning ch lp; CL in lp; ch 1, dc in 3rd ch of turning ch-4; ch 4, turn.

Row 6: CL in next ch-1 sp; shell in next shell; * ch 5, sk next ch-4 lp, sc in next ch-4 lp, (ch 4, sc in next ch-4 lp) twice; ch 5, shell in each of next 3 shells; rep from * across to turning ch lp; CL in lp; ch 1, dc in 3rd ch of turning ch-4; ch 4, turn.

Row 7: CL in next ch-1 sp; shell in next shell; * ch 6, sc in next ch-4 lp, ch 4, sc in next ch-4 lp, ch 6, shell in each of next 3 shells; rep from * across to turning ch lp; CL in lp; ch 1, dc in 3rd ch of turning ch-4; ch 4, turn.

Row 8: CL in next ch-1 sp; shell in next shell; * ch 7, sc in next ch-4 lp, ch 7, shell in each of next 3 shells; rep from * across to turning ch lp; CL in lp; ch 1, dc in 3rd ch of turning ch-4; ch 4, turn.

Row 9: CL in next ch-1 sp; shell in next shell; * ch 3, sc in next ch-7 lp, ch 5, sc in next ch-7 lp, ch 3, shell in each of next 3 shells; rep from * across to turning ch lp; CL in lp; ch 1, dc in 3rd ch of turning ch-4; ch 4, turn.

Row 10: CL in next ch-1 sp; shell in next shell; * ch 3, 6 dc in next ch-5 lp; ch 3, shell in each of next 3 shells; rep from * across to turning ch lp; CL in lp; ch 1, dc in 3rd ch of turning ch-4; ch 4, turn.

Rep Rows 3 through 10 for pattern.

#64

Multiple of 6 + 2

PATTERN STITCH

Cluster (CL): Keeping last lp of each dc on hook, 2 dc in next sp, YO and draw through all 3 lps on hook: CL made.

Row 1: Sc in 2nd ch from hook; * ch 2, sk next 2 chs, in next ch work (dc, ch 2, dc); ch 2, sk next 2 chs, sc in next ch; rep from * across; ch 4, turn.

Row 2 (right side): Sk next ch-2 sp; * in next ch-2 sp work [CL (see Pattern Stitch), ch 1] 3 times; sk next 2 ch-2 sps; rep from * across to last ch-2 sp; sk last ch-2 sp, trc in last sc; ch 1, turn.

Row 3: Sc in next trc; * ch 1, sc in next ch-1 sp; rep from * across to last trc; sc in 4th ch of turning ch-4; ch 3, turn.

Row 4: * Dc in next ch-1 sp, ch 1; rep from * across to last sc; dc in last sc; ch 1, turn.

Row 5: Sc in next dc; * ch 2, sk next dc, in next dc work (dc, ch 2, dc); ch 2, sk next ch-1 sp, sc in next ch-1 sp; rep from * across to turning ch; sc in 3rd ch of turning ch-3; ch 4, turn.

Rep Rows 2 through 5 for pattern.

#65

Multiple of 12 + 2

PATTERN STITCH

Cluster (CL): YO, draw up lp in next dc, YO, draw up lp in same dc; YO and draw through all 5 lps on hook: CL made.

Row 1 (right side): Sc in 2nd ch from hook and in next 3 chs, sk next 2 chs, 6 dc in next ch; * sk next 2 chs, sc in next 7 chs, sk next 2 chs, 6 dc in next ch; rep from * across to last 6 chs; sk next 2 chs, sc in last 4 chs; ch 1, turn.

Row 2: Sc in next sc; * CL (see Pattern Stitch) in next dc; ch 1, (CL in next dc, ch 1) 5 times; sk next 3 sc, sc in next sc; sk next 3 sc; rep from * across to last 4 sc; sk next 3 sc, sc in last sc; ch 3, turn.

Row 3: 2 dc in first sc; * sk next ch-1 sp, sc in next ch-1 sp, ch 7, sk next 3 ch-1 sps, sc in next ch-1 sp, 6 dc in next sc; rep from * across to last sc; 3 dc in last sc; ch 3, turn.

Row 4: Dc in first dc, ch 1, (CL in next dc, ch 1) twice; * working over next ch-7 lp, sc in 2nd skipped ch-1 sp in 2nd row below, (CL in next dc, ch 1) 6 times; rep from * across to turning ch; 2 dc in 3rd ch of turning ch-3; ch 1, turn.

Row 5: Sc in next dc, ch 3, sk next ch-1 sp; * sc in next ch-1 sp, 6 dc in next sc; sk next ch-1 sp, sc in next ch-1 sp, ch 7, sk next 3 ch-1 sps; rep from * across to last 3 ch-1 sps; sk next ch-1 sp, sc in next ch-1 sp, ch 3, sk last ch-1 sp, sc in 3rd ch of turning ch-3; ch 1, turn.

Row 6: Sc in next sc; * (CL in next dc, ch 1) 6 times; working over next ch-7 lp, sc in 2nd skipped ch-1 sp in 2nd row below; rep from * across to last sc; sc in last sc; ch 3, turn.

Rep Rows 3 through 6 for pattern.

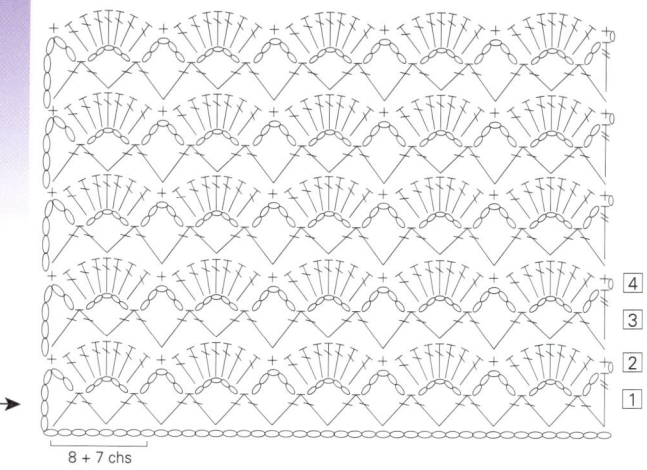

8 + 7 chs

#66

Multiple of 8 + 7

> **PATTERN STITCH**
>
> **Cluster** (CL): Keeping last lp of each dc on hook, dc in same st as last dc made, sk next 3 sts, dc in next st, YO and draw through all 3 lps on hook: CL made.

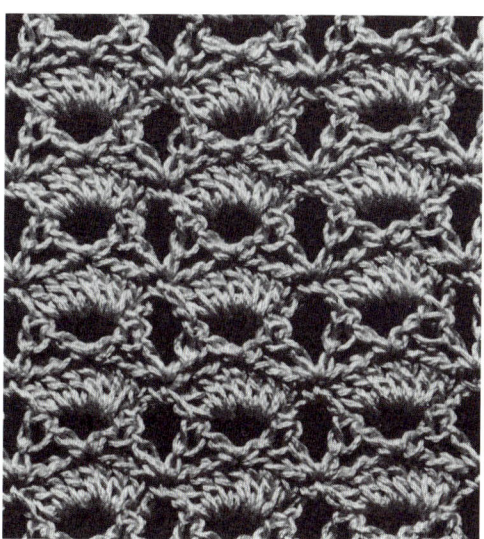

Row 1: Keeping last lp of each dc on hook, dc in 7th ch from hook, sk next 3 chs, dc in next ch, YO and draw through all 3 lps on hook; * ch 5, CL (see Pattern Stitch) over same ch as last dc made and next 4 chs; rep from * across; ch 2, trc in same ch as last dc made; ch 1, turn.

Row 2 (right side): Sc in next trc, 7 dc in next ch-5 lp; * sc in next ch-5 lp, 7 dc in next ch-5 lp; rep from * across to lp formed by beg 6 skipped chs; sc in lp; ch 6, turn.

Row 3: Keeping last lp of each dc on hook, dc in first sc, sk next 3 dc, dc in next dc, YO and draw through all 3 lps on hook; * ch 5, CL; rep from * across; ch 2, trc in same sc as last dc made; ch 1, turn.

Row 4: Sc in next trc, 7 dc in next ch-5 lp; * sc in next ch-5 lp, 7 dc in next ch-5 lp; rep from * across to turning ch lp; sc in lp; ch 6, turn.

Rep Rows 3 and 4 for pattern.

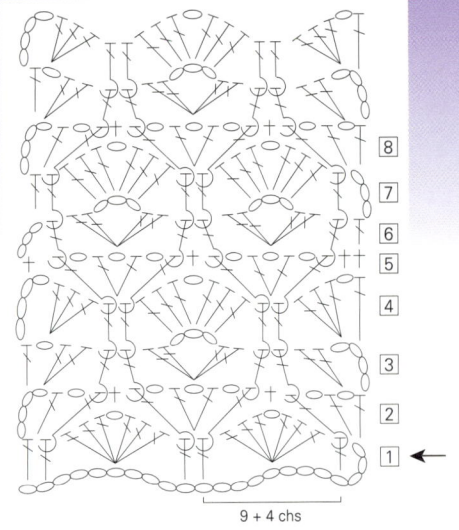

9 + 4 chs

#67

Muliple of 9 + 4

> **PATTERN STITCHES**
>
> **Front Post Double Crochet** (FPdc): YO, insert hook from front to back to front around post (see page 8) of next dc, YO and draw lp through, (YO and draw through 2 lps on hook) twice: FPdc made.
>
> **Back Post Double Crochet** (BPdc): YO, insert hook from back to front to back around post (see page 8) of next dc, YO and draw lp through, (YO and draw through 2 lps on hook) twice: BPdc made.

Row 1 (right side): Dc in 4th ch from hook; * sk next 3 chs, in next ch work (3 dc, ch 1, 3 dc); sk next 3 chs, dc in next 2 chs; rep from * across; ch 4, turn.

Row 2: Dc in first dc, ch 1, BPdc (see Pattern Stitches) around post of next dc; * sc in next ch-1 sp, sk next 3 dc, BPdc around post of next dc; ch 1, in sp between last dc worked and next dc work (dc, ch 1, dc); ch 1, BPdc around post of next dc; rep from * across to last dc; BPdc around post of last dc; ch 1, dc between last dc worked and beg 3 skipped chs, ch 1, dc in 3rd ch of 3 skipped chs; ch 4, turn.

Row 3: 2 dc in next ch-1 sp; * sk next dc, FPdc (see Pattern Stitches) around post of next BPdc; sk next sc, FPdc around post of next BPdc; sk next ch-1 sp, in next ch-1 sp work (2 dc, ch 3, 2 dc); rep from * across to turning ch lp; 2 dc in lp; ch 1, dc in 3rd ch of turning ch-4; ch 4, turn.

Row 4: 3 dc in next ch-1 sp; * BPdc around each of next 2 FPdc; in next ch-3-lp work (3 dc, ch 1, 3 dc); rep from * across to last 2 FPdc; BPdc around each of last 2 FPdc; 3 dc in turning ch lp; ch 1, dc in 3rd ch of turning ch-4; ch 1, turn.

Row 5: Sc in next dc and in next ch-1 sp; * FPdc around next BPdc; ch 1, in sp between last BPdc and next BPdc work (dc, ch 1, dc); ch 1, FPdc around next BPdc; sc in next ch-1 sp; rep from * across to turning ch; sc in 3rd ch of turning ch-4; ch 3, turn.

Row 6: * BPdc around next FPdc; sk next ch-1 sp, in next ch-1 sp work (2 dc, ch 3, 2 dc); BPdc around next FPdc; sk next sc; rep from * across to last sc; dc in last sc; ch 3, turn.

Row 7: FPdc around next BPdc; * in next ch-3 lp work (3 dc, ch 1, 3 dc); FPdc around each of next 2 BPdc; rep from * across to turning ch; dc in 3rd ch of turning ch-3; ch 4, turn.

Row 8: Dc in first dc, ch 1, BPdc around next FPdc; * sc in next ch-1 sp, sk next 3 dc, BPdc around next FPdc; ch 1, in sp between last dc and next dc work (dc, ch 1, dc); ch 1, BPdc around next FPdc; rep from * across to last FPdc; BPdc around last FPdc; ch 1, dc between last dc and turning ch, ch 1, dc in 3rd ch of turning ch-3; ch 4, turn.

Rep Rows 3 through 8 for pattern.

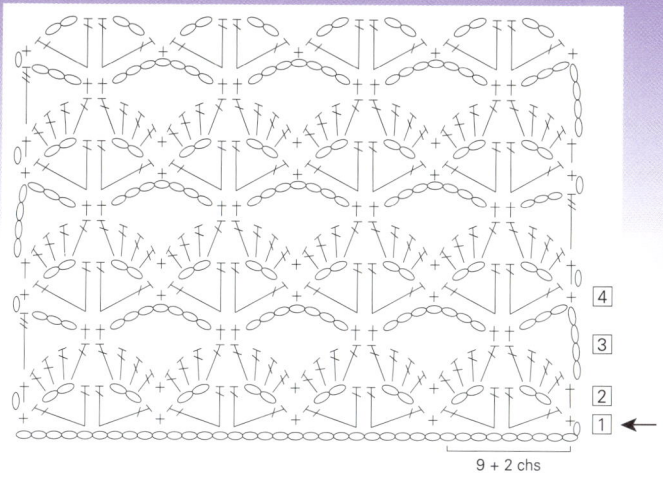

#68

Multiple of 9 + 2

Row 1 (right side): Sc in 2nd ch from hook; * sk next 3 chs, in each of next 2 chs work (dc, ch 2, dc); sk next 3 chs, sc in next ch; rep from * across; ch 1, turn.

Row 2: Sc in next sc; * 4 dc in each of next 2 ch-2 sps; sc in next sc; rep from * across; ch 7, turn.

Row 3: Sk next 3 dc; * sc in next 2 dc, ch 7, sk next 7 sts; rep from * across to last sc; ch 3, trc in last sc; ch 1, turn.

Row 4: Sc in next trc; * in each of next 2 sc work (dc, ch 2, dc); sc in next ch-7 lp; rep from * across to turning ch; sc in 4th ch of turning ch-7; ch 1, turn.

Rep Rows 2 through 4 for pattern.

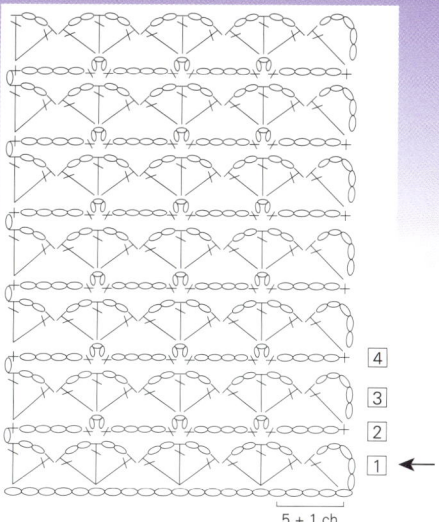

#69

Multiple of 5 + 1

Row 1 (right side): Dc in 6th ch from hook, sk next 4 chs; * in next ch work (dc, ch 2, dc, ch 2, dc); sk next 4 chs; rep from * across to last ch; in last ch work (dc, ch 2, dc); ch 1, turn.

Row 2: Sc in next dc, ch 4, sk next 2 dc; * in next dc work (sc, ch 3, sc); ch 4, sk next 2 dc; rep from * across to beg 5 skipped chs; sc in 3rd ch of 5 skipped chs; ch 5, turn.

Row 3: Dc in next sc, sk next ch-4 lp; * in next ch-3 lp work (dc, ch 2, dc, ch 2, dc); rep from * across to last sc; in last sc work (dc, ch 2, dc); ch 1, turn.

Row 4: Sc in next dc, ch 4, sk next 2 dc; * in next dc work (sc, ch 3, sc); ch 4, sk next 2 dc; rep from * across to turning ch; sc in 3rd ch of turning ch-5; ch 5, turn.

Rep Rows 3 and 4 for pattern.

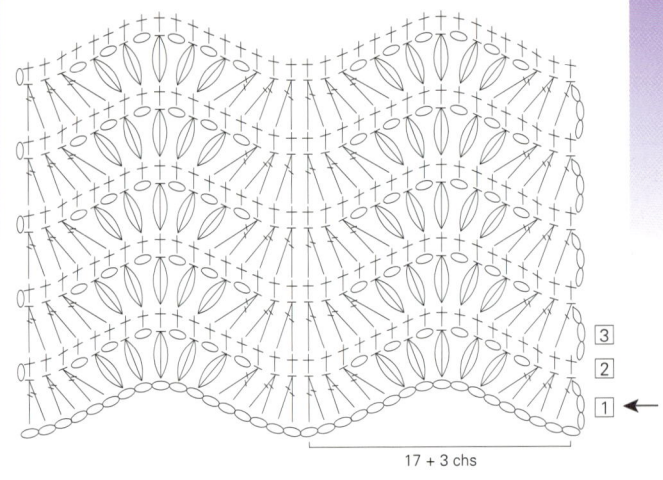

#70

Multiple of 17 + 3

> **PATTERN STITCH**
>
> **Cluster** (CL): YO, draw up lp in next st, (YO, draw up lp in same st) twice; YO, draw through all 7 lps on hook: CL made.

Row 1 (right side): Dc in 5th ch from hook, dec over next 2 chs (to work dec: keeping last lp of each dc on hook, dc in next 2 sts, YO and draw through all 3 lps on hook: dec made); dec over next 2 chs; ch 1, [CL (see Pattern Stitch) in next ch, ch 1] 5 times; * (dec over next 2 chs) 6 times; ch 1, (CL in next ch, ch 1) 5 times; rep from * across to last 6 chs; (dec over next 2 chs) 3 times; ch 1, turn.

Row 2: Sc in each st and in each ch across to last dc; sc in last dc; ch 3 (counts as first dc on following rows), turn.

Row 3: Dc in next sc, dec twice; * ch 1, (CL in next sc, ch 1) 5 times; dec 6 times; rep from * across to last 6 sc; dec 3 times; ch 1, turn.

Rep Rows 2 and 3 for pattern.

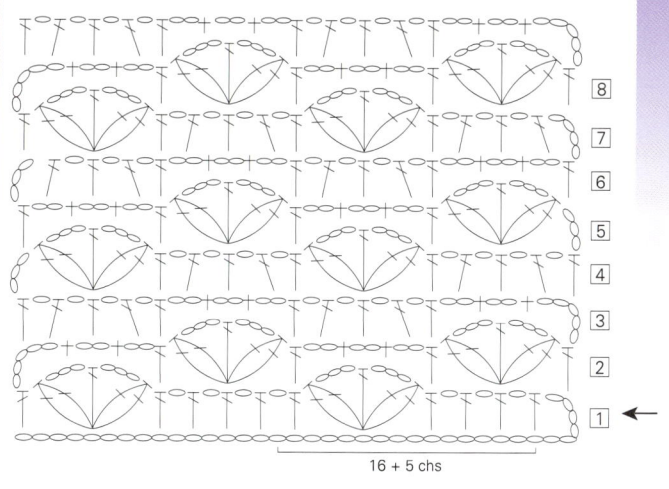

#71

Multiple of 16 + 5

> **PATTERN STITCH**
> **Cluster** (CL): Keeping last lp of each dc on hook, 2 dc in st, YO and draw through all 3 lps on hook: CL made.

Row 1 (right side): Dc in 7th ch from hook, (ch 1, sk next ch, dc in next ch) 3 times; sk next 3 chs, in next ch work [CL (see Pattern Stitch), ch 3, dc, ch 3, CL]; * sk next 3 chs, dc in next ch, (ch 1, sk next ch, dc in next ch) 4 times; sk next 3 chs, in next ch work (CL, ch 3, dc, ch 3, CL); rep from * across to last 4 chs; sk next 3 chs, dc in last ch; ch 5, turn.

Row 2: * (Sc in next ch-3 lp, ch 2) twice; dc in next dc, sk next dc, in next dc work (CL, ch 3, dc, ch 3, CL); sk next dc, dc in next dc, ch 2; rep from * across to beg 6 skipped chs; dc in 5th ch of 6 skipped chs; ch 5, turn.

Row 3: * (Sc in next ch-3 lp, ch 2) twice; dc in next dc, (ch 1, dc in next ch-2 sp) 3 times; ch 1, dc in next dc, ch 2; rep from * across to turning ch lp; dc in lp, ch 1, dc in 3rd ch of turning ch-5; ch 3, turn.

Row 4: Sk first 2 dc; * in next dc work (CL, ch 3, dc, ch 3, CL); sk next dc, dc in next dc, (ch 1, dc in next ch-2 sp) 3 times; ch 1, dc in next dc, sk next dc; rep from * across to turning ch lp; dc in lp, ch 1, dc in 3rd ch of turning ch-5; ch 3, turn.

Row 5: Sk first 2 dc; * in next dc work (CL, ch 3, dc, ch 3, CL); sk next dc, dc in next dc, (ch 2, sc in next ch-3 lp) twice; ch 2, dc in next dc, sk next dc; rep from * across to turning ch; dc in 3rd ch of turning ch-3; ch 3, turn.

Row 6: * (Dc in next ch-2 sp, ch 1) 3 times; dc in next dc, (ch 2, sc in next ch-2 sp) twice; ch 2, dc in next dc, ch 1; rep from * across to turning ch; dc in 3rd ch of turning ch-3; ch 4, turn.

Row 7: * (Dc in next ch-2 sp, ch 1) 3 times; dc in next dc, sk next dc, in next dc work (CL, ch 3, dc, ch 3, CL); sk next dc, dc in next dc, ch 1; rep from * across to turning ch; dc in 3rd ch of turning ch-3; ch 5, turn.

Row 8: * (Sc in next ch-3 lp, ch 2) twice; dc in next dc, sk next dc, in next dc work (CL, ch 3, dc, ch 3, CL); sk next dc, dc in next dc, ch 2; rep from * across to turning ch; dc in 3rd ch of turning ch-4; ch 5, turn.

Rep Rows 3 through 8 for pattern.

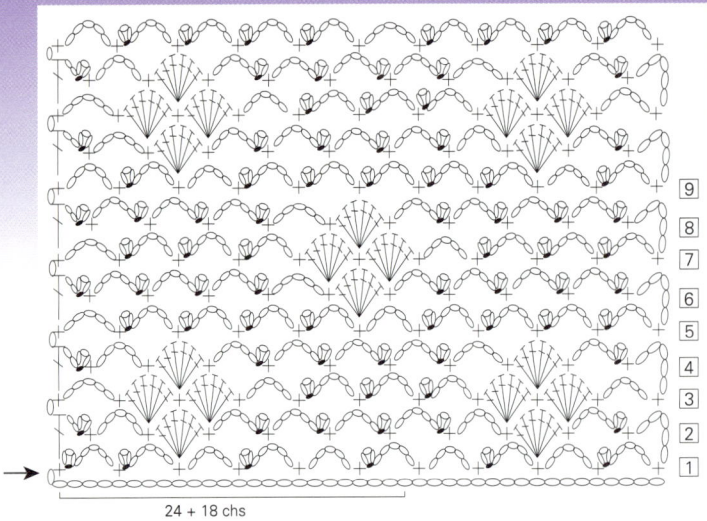

24 + 18 chs

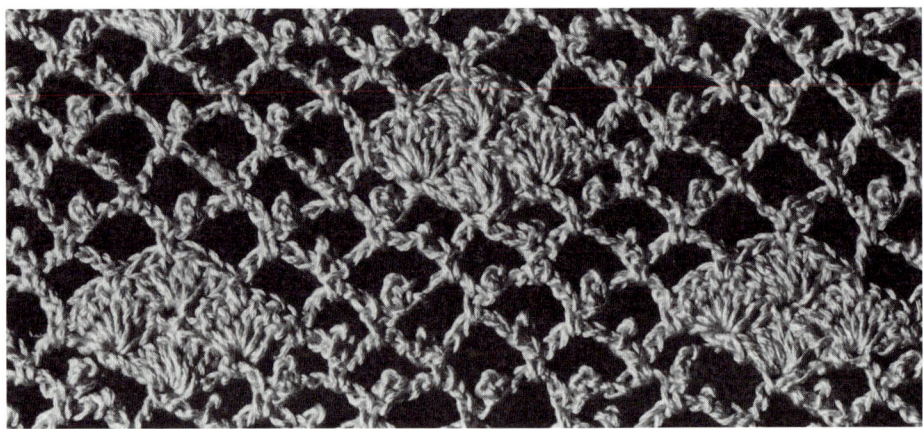

#72

Multiple of 24 + 18

Row 1: Sc in 2nd ch from hook; ch 3, sl st in first ch: picot made; ch 5, sk next 3 chs, sc in next ch, picot; * ch 5, sk next 3 chs, sc in next ch, ch 5, sk next 3 chs, sc in next ch, picot; rep from * across to last 4 chs; ch 5, sk next 3 chs, sc in last ch; ch 5, turn.

Row 2 (right side): Sc in next ch-5 lp, picot; ch 5, sc in next ch-5 lp, 6 dc in next sc; sc in next ch-5 lp; * (ch 5, sc in next ch-5 lp, picot) 4 times; ch 5, sc in next ch-5 lp, 6 dc in next sc; sc in next ch-5 lp; rep from * across to last ch-5 lp; ch 5, sc in last ch-5 lp, picot; ch 2, dc in last sc; ch 1, turn.

Row 3: Sc in next dc, ch 5, sc in next ch-5 lp, 6 dc in next sc; sk next 2 dc, sc between next 2 dc, 6 dc in next sc; sc in next ch-5 lp, ch 5; * (sc in next ch-5 lp, picot, ch 5) 3 times; sc in next ch-5 lp, 6 dc in next sc; sk next 2 dc, sc between next 2 dc, 6 dc in next sc; sc in next ch-5 lp, ch 5; rep from * across to turning ch lp; sc in lp; ch 5, turn.

Row 4: Sc in next ch-5 lp, picot; ch 5, sk next 2 dc, sc between next 2 dc, 6 dc in next sc; sk next 2 dc, sc between next 2 dc, ch 5; * (sc in next ch-5 lp, picot, ch 5) 4 times; sk next 2 dc, sc between next 2 dc, 6 dc in next sc; sk next 2 dc, sc between next 2 dc, ch 5; rep from * across to last ch-5 lp; sc in last ch-5 lp, picot; ch 2, dc in last sc; ch 1, turn.

Row 5: Sc in next dc, ch 5, sc in next ch-5 lp, picot; ch 5, sk next 2 dc, sc between next 2 dc, picot; ch 5; * (sc in next ch-5 lp, picot, ch 5) twice; sc in next ch-5 lp, (ch 5, sc in next ch-5 lp, picot) twice; ch 5, sk next

2 dc, sc between next 2 dc, picot; ch 5; rep from * across to last ch-5 lp; sc in last ch-5 lp, picot; ch 5, sc in turning ch lp; ch 5, turn.

Row 6: (Sc in next ch-5 lp, picot, ch 5) 4 times; * sc in next ch-5 lp, 6 dc in next sc; sc in next ch-5 lp, (ch 5, sc in next ch-5 lp, picot) 4 times; ch 5; rep from * across to last sc; ch 2, dc in last sc; ch 1, turn.

Row 7: Sc in next dc, ch 5, (sc in next ch-5 lp, picot, ch 5) 3 times; * sc in next ch-5 lp, 6 dc in next sc; sk next 3 dc, sc between next 2 dc, 6 dc in next sc; sc in next ch-5 lp, (ch 5, sc in next ch-4 lp, picot) 3 times; ch 5; rep from * across to turning ch lp; sc in lp; ch 5, turn.

Row 8: (Sc in next ch-5 lp, picot, ch 5) 4 times; * sk next 2 dc, sc between next 2 dc, 6 dc in next sc; sk next 2 dc, sc between next 2 dc, (ch 5, sc in next ch-5 lp, picot) 4 times; ch 5; rep from * across to last sc; ch 2, dc in last sc; ch 1, turn.

Row 9: Sc in next dc, ch 5, sc in next ch-5 lp, picot; ch 5, sc in next ch-5 lp; * (ch 5, sc in next ch-5 lp, picot) twice; ch 5, sk next 2 dc, sc between next 2 dc, picot; (ch 5, sc in next ch-5 lp, picot) twice; ch 5, sc in next ch-5 lp; rep from * across to turning ch lp; ch 5, sc in lp; ch 5, turn.

Rep Rows 2 through 9 for pattern.

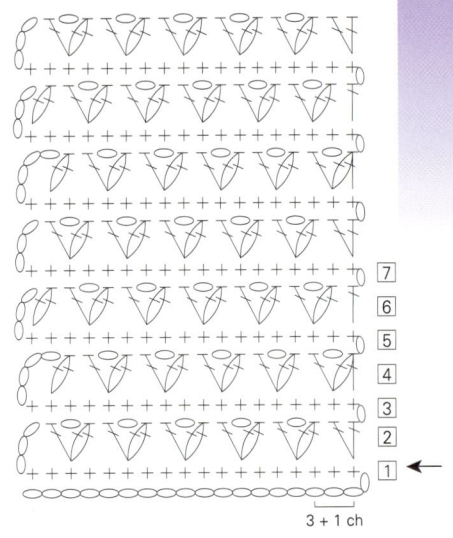

#73

Multiple of 3 + 1

> **PATTERN STITCH**
>
> **Cluster** (CL): Keeping last lp of each dc on hook, 2 dc in st, YO and draw through all 3 lps on hook: CL made.

Row 1 (right side): Sc in 2nd ch from hook and in each rem ch; ch 3 (counts as first dc on following rows), turn.

Row 2: Sk next sc; * in next sc work [dc, ch 1, CL (see Pattern Stitch)]; sk next 2 sc; rep from * across to last sc; 2 dc in last sc; ch 1, turn.

Row 3: Sc in each dc, in each CL, and in each ch-1 sp across to turning ch; sc in 3rd ch of turning ch-3; ch 4 (counts as first dc and ch-1 sp on following rows), turn.

Row 4: CL in next sc; * sk next 2 sc, in next sc work (dc, ch 1, CL); rep from * across to last 4 sc; sk next 2 sc, dc in next sc, ch 1, keeping last lp of each dc on hook, 2 dc in same sc as last dc made, dc in last sc; YO and draw through all 4 lps on hook: joined CL made; ch 1, turn.

Row 5: Sc in next joined CL, sc in each ch-1 sp, in each dc, and in each CL across to turning ch; sc in 3rd and 4th chs of turning ch-4; ch 3, turn.

Row 6: CL in first sc; * sk next 2 sc, in next sc work (dc, ch 1, CL); rep from * across to last 2 sc; sk next sc, dc in last sc; ch 1, turn.

Row 7: Sc in each dc, in each CL and in each ch-1 sp across to turning ch; sc in 3rd ch of turning ch-3; ch 3, turn.

Rep Rows 2 through 7 for pattern.

14 + 2 chs

#74

Multiple of 14 + 2

PATTERN STITCHES

Cluster (CL): Keeping last lp of each dc on hook, 3 dc in next lp, YO and draw through all 4 lps on hook: CL made.

2-dc Cluster (2-dc CL): Keeping last lp of each dc on hook, 2 dc in next st, YO and draw through all 3 lps on hook: 2-dc CL made.

Row 1 (right side): Sc in 2nd ch from hook and in next 3 chs; * ch 2, sk next 3 chs, in next ch work [CL (see Pattern Stitches), ch 2] 4 times; sk next 3 chs, sc in next 7 chs; rep from * across to last 4 sc; sc in last 4 sc; ch 1, turn.

Row 2: * Sc in next sc, ch 2, sk next ch-2 sp, in each of next 2 ch-2 sps work (dc, ch 1) 3 times; in next ch-2 sp work (dc, ch 1, dc, ch 1, dc); ch 2, sk next 3 sc; rep from * across to last sc; sc in last sc; ch 3, turn.

Row 3: Dc in first sc; * ch 2, sk next ch-1 sp, (sc in next ch-1 sp, ch 2) 6 times; in next sc work (dc, ch 1, dc); rep from * across to last sc; 2 dc in last sc; ch 4, turn.

Row 4: 2-dc CL (see Pattern Stitches) in first dc; * ch 2, sk next ch-2 sp, (sc in next ch-2 sp, ch 2) 5 times; in next ch-1 sp work (2-dc CL, ch 2, 2-dc CL); rep from * across to turning ch; in 3rd ch of turning ch-3 work (2-dc CL, ch 1, dc); ch 4, turn.

Row 5: In next ch-1 sp work (CL, ch 2) twice; * sk next ch-2 sp, (sc in next ch-2 sp and in next sc) 3 times; sc in next ch-2 sp, ch 2, sk next ch-2 sp, in next ch-2 sp work (CL, ch 2) 4 times; rep from * across to turning ch lp; in lp work (CL, ch 2, CL); ch 1, dc in 3rd ch of turning ch-4; ch 4, turn.

Row 6: Dc in next ch-1 sp, ch 1; * in next ch-2 sp work (dc, ch 1, dc, ch 1, dc); ch 2, sk next 3 sc, sc in next sc, ch 2, sk next ch-2 sp, in each of next 2 ch-2 sps work (dc, ch 1) 3 times; rep from * across to last ch-2 sp; in last ch-2 sp work (dc, ch 1) 3 times; dc in turning ch lp, ch 1, dc in 3rd ch of turning ch-4; ch 3, turn.

Row 7: (Sc in next ch-1 sp, ch 2) 3 times; * in next sc work (dc, ch 1, dc); ch 2, sk next ch-1 sp, (sc in next ch-1 sp, ch 2) 6 times; rep from * across to last 2 ch-1 sps; (sc in next ch-1 sp, ch 2) twice; sc in turning ch lp, ch 1, hdc in 3rd ch of turning ch-4; ch 1, turn.

Row 8: Sc in next hdc, (ch 2, sc in next ch-2 sp) twice; ch 2; * in next ch-1 sp work (2-dc CL, ch 2, 2-dc CL); ch 2, sk next ch-2 sp, (sc in next ch-2 sp, ch 2) 5 times; rep from * across to last 2 ch-2 sps; (sc in next ch-2 sp, ch 2) twice; sc in 2nd ch of turning ch-3; ch 1, turn.

Row 9: (Sc in next sc and in next ch-2 sp) twice; * ch 2, sk next ch-2 sp, in next ch-2 sp work (CL, ch 2) 4 times; sk next ch-2 sp, (sc in next ch-2 sp and in next sc) 3 times; sc in next ch-2 sp; rep from * across to last 2 ch-2 sps; (sc in next ch-2 sp and in next sc) twice; ch 1, turn.

Rep Rows 2 through 9 for pattern.

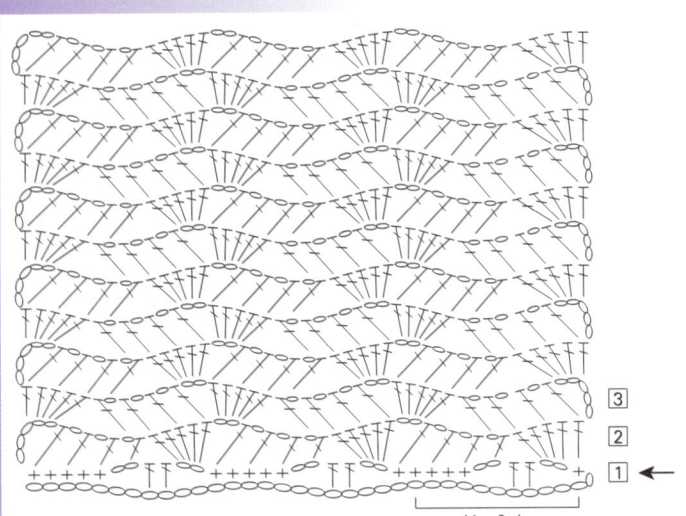

11 + 2 chs

6 + 2 chs

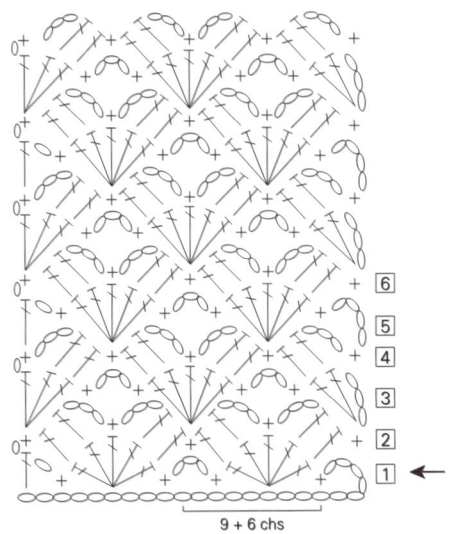

9 + 6 chs

#75

Multiple of 11 + 2

Row 1 (right side): Sc in 2nd ch from hook; * ch 2, sk next 2 chs, dc in next 2 chs, ch 2, sk next 2 chs, sc in next 5 chs; rep from * across; ch 5, turn.

Row 2: Dc in first sc; * (ch 1, sk next sc, dc in next sc) twice; ch 1, dc in next ch-2 sp, 5 dc in next ch-2 sp; ch 2, dc in next sc; rep from * across to last ch-2 sp; 4 dc in last ch-2 sp, dc in last sc; ch 5, turn.

Row 3: Dc in first dc, (ch 1, sk next dc, dc in next dc) twice; ch 1; * dc in next ch-1 sp, 5 dc in next ch-2 sp; ch 2, (dc in next dc, ch 1, sk next dc) 3 times; rep from * across to turning ch lp; 4 dc in lp; dc in 3rd ch of turning ch-5; ch 5, turn.

Rep Row 3 for pattern.

#76

Multiple of 6 + 2

> **PATTERN STITCH**
>
> **Cluster** (CL): Keeping last lp of each trc on hook, 5 trc in next sc, YO and draw through all 6 lps on hook: CL made.

Row 1: Sc in 2nd ch from hook and in each rem ch; ch 3, turn.

Row 2 (right side): 2 dc in first sc; * sk next 2 sc, sc in next sc, sk next 2 sc, 5 dc in next sc; rep from * across to last sc; 3 dc in last sc; ch 1, turn.

Row 3: Sc in next dc; * ch 3, CL (see Pattern Stitch) in next sc; ch 3, sk next 2 dc, sc in next dc; rep from * across to last 2 dc; ch 3, sk next 2 dc, sc in 3rd ch of turning ch-3; ch 3, turn.

Row 4: 2 dc in first sc; * sc in next CL, 5 dc in next sc; rep from * across to last sc; 3 dc in last sc; ch 1, turn.

Rep Rows 3 and 4 for pattern.

#77

Multiple of 9 + 6

Row 1 (right side): Sc in 7th ch from hook; * sk next 2 chs, 5 dc in next ch; sk next 2 chs, sc in next ch, ch 3, sk next 2 chs, sc in next ch; rep from * across to last 2 chs; ch 1, sk next ch, dc in last ch; ch 1, turn.

Row 2: Sc in next dc; * dc in next 2 dc, ch 3, sc in next dc, ch 3, dc in next 2 dc, sc in next ch-3 lp; rep from * across to beg 6 skipped chs; sc in 4th ch of 6 skipped chs; ch 3, turn.

Row 3: 2 dc in first sc; * sc in next ch-3 lp, ch 3, sc in next ch-3 lp, 5 dc in next sc; rep from * across to last sc; 3 dc in last sc; ch 1, turn.

Row 4: Sc in next dc; * ch 3, dc in next 2 dc, sc in next ch-3 lp, dc in next 2 dc, ch 3, sc in next dc; rep from * across to turning ch; sc in 3rd ch of turning ch-3; ch 4, turn.

Row 5: * Sc in next ch-3 lp, 5 dc in next sc; sc in next ch-3 lp, ch 3; rep from * across to last sc; ch 1, dc in last sc; ch 1, turn.

Row 6: Sc in next dc; * dc in next 2 dc, ch 3, sc in next dc, ch 3, dc in next 2 dc, sc in next ch-3 lp; rep from * across to turning ch; sc in 3rd ch of turning ch-4; ch 3, turn.

Rep Rows 3 through 6 for pattern.

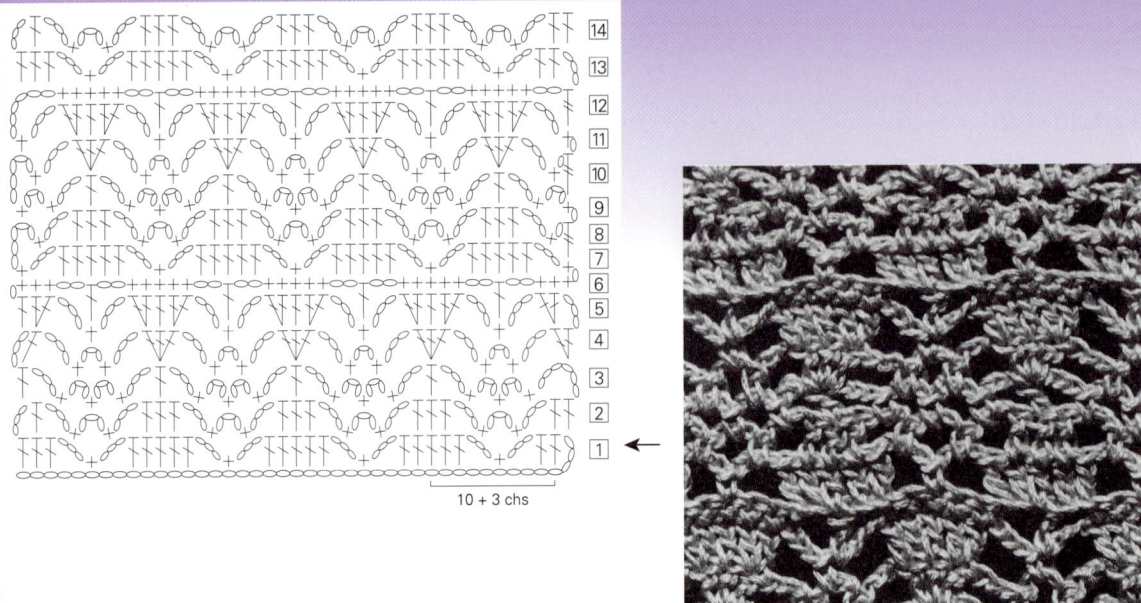

#78

Multiple of 10 + 3

Row 1 (right side): Dc in 4th ch from hook and in next ch; * ch 3, sk next 2 chs, sc in next ch, ch 3, sk next 2 chs, dc in next 5 chs; rep from * across to last 3 chs; dc in last 3 chs; ch 3 (counts as first dc on following rows), turn.

Row 2: Dc in next dc, (ch 3, sc in next ch-3 lp) twice; ch 3, sk next dc, dc in next 3 dc, ch 3; * sc in next ch-3 lp, ch 3, sc in next ch-3 lp, ch 3, sk next dc, dc in next 3 dc, ch 3; rep from * across to last 2 dc; sk next dc, dc in last dc and in 3rd ch of beg 4 skipped chs; ch 6, turn.

Row 3: Sc in next ch-3 lp, (ch 3, sc in next ch-3 lp) twice; ch 3, sk next dc, dc in next dc; * (ch 3, sc in next ch-3 lp) 3 times; ch 3, sk next dc, dc in next dc; rep from * across to turning ch; ch 3, dc in 3rd ch of turning ch-3; ch 3, turn.

Row 4: Dc in first dc; * ch 3, sk next ch-3 lp, (sc in next ch-3 lp, ch 3) twice; 3 dc in next dc; rep from * across to turning ch; 2 dc in 3rd ch of turning ch-6; ch 3, turn.

Row 5: 2 dc in next dc; ch 3, sk next ch-3 lp, sc in next ch-3 lp, ch 3; * 2 dc in next dc; dc in next dc, 2 dc in next dc; ch 3, sk next ch-3 lp, sc in next ch-3 lp, ch 3; rep from * across to last dc; 2 dc in last dc; dc in 3rd ch of turning ch-3; ch 1, turn.

Row 6: Sc in next 3 dc, ch 2, dc in next sc, ch 2; * sc in next 5 dc, ch 2, dc in next sc, ch 2; rep from * across to last 2 dc; sc in last 2 dc and in 3rd ch of turning ch-3; ch 1, turn.

Row 7: Sc in next sc, ch 3, dc in next 2 chs, in next dc, and in next 2 chs; * ch 3, sk next 2 sc, sc in next sc, ch 3, dc in next 2 chs, in next dc, and in next 2 chs; rep from * across to last 3 sc; ch 3, sk next 2 sc, sc in last sc; ch 5, turn.

Row 8: Sc in next ch-3 lp, ch 3, sk next dc, dc in next 3 dc; * (ch 3, sc in next ch-3 lp) twice; ch 3, sk next dc, dc in next 3 dc; rep from * across to last ch-3 lp; ch 3, sc in last ch-3 lp, ch 1, trc in last sc; ch 1, turn.

Row 9: Sc in next trc, ch 3, sc in next ch-3 lp, ch 3, sk next dc, dc in next dc, ch 3; * (sc in next ch-3 lp, ch 3) 3 times; sk next dc, dc in next dc, ch 3; rep from * across to last ch-3 lp; sc in last ch-3 lp, ch 3, sc in 4th ch of turning ch-5; ch 5, turn.

Row 10: Sc in next ch-3 lp, ch 3; * 3 dc in next dc; ch 3, sk next ch-3 lp, (sc in next ch-3 lp, ch 3) twice; rep from * across to last ch-3 lp; sc in last ch-3 lp, ch 1, trc in last sc; ch 1, turn.

Row 11: Sc in next trc, ch 3, 2 dc in next dc; dc in next dc, 2 dc in next dc; ch 3, sk next ch-3 lp; * sc in next ch-3 lp, ch 3, 2 dc in next dc; dc in next dc, 2 dc in next dc; ch 3, sk next ch-3 lp; rep from * across to turning ch; sc in 4th ch of turning ch-5; ch 6, turn.

Row 12: Sc in next 5 dc; * ch 2, dc in next sc, ch 2, sc in next 5 dc; rep from * across to last sc; ch 2, trc in last sc; ch 3, turn.

Row 13: Dc in next 2 chs, ch 3, sk next 2 sc, sc in next sc, ch 3, sk next 2 sc; * dc in next 2 chs, in next dc, and in next 2 chs; ch 3, sk next 2 sc, sc in next sc, ch 3, sk next 2 sc; rep from * across to turning ch; dc in next 3 chs of turning ch-6; ch 3, turn.

Row 14: Dc in next dc, (ch 3, sc in next ch-3 lp) twice; ch 3, sk next dc, dc in next 3 dc; * (ch 3, sc in next ch-3 lp) twice; ch 3, sk next dc, dc in next 3 dc; rep from * across to last 2 dc; sk next dc, dc in last dc and in 3rd ch of turning ch-3; ch 6, turn.

Rep Rows 3 through 14 for pattern.

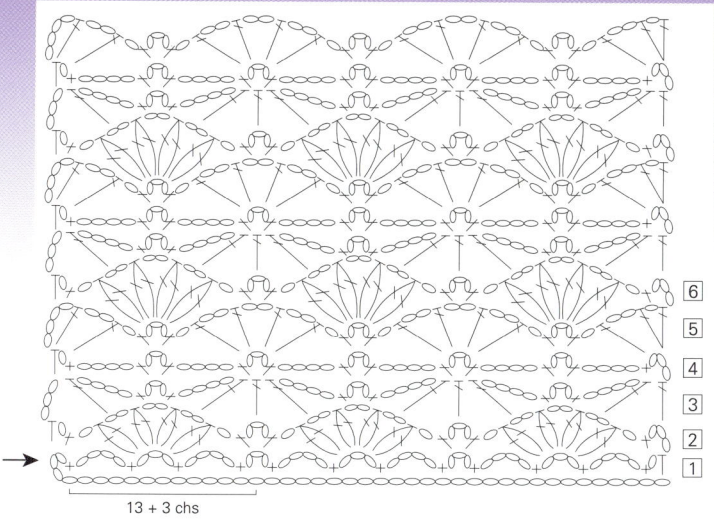

#79

Multiple of 13 + 3

> **PATTERN STITCH**
>
> **Cluster** (CL): Keeping last lp of each dc on hook, 2 dc in lp, YO and draw through all 3 lps on hook: CL made.

Row 1: Sc in 4th ch from hook; * ch 4, sk next 3 chs, sc in next ch, ch 3, sk next 2 chs, sc in next ch, ch 4, sk next 3 chs, sc in next ch, ch 3, sk next ch, sc in next ch; rep from * across to last ch; ch 1, hdc in last ch; ch 3, turn.

Row 2 (right side): Sc in next ch-1 sp; * ch 1, in next ch-3 lp work [CL (see Pattern Stitch), ch 2] 3 times; CL in same lp; ch 1, sk next ch-4 lp, in next ch-3 lp work (sc, ch 3, sc); rep from * across to lp formed by beg 3 skipped chs; sc in lp, ch 1, hdc in 2nd ch of 3 skipped chs; ch 3, turn.

Row 3: Dc in next ch-2 sp; * ch 4, in next ch-2 sp work (sc, ch 3, sc); ch 4, dc in next ch-2 sp, in next ch-3 lp, and in next ch-2 sp; rep from * across to turning ch; dc in 2nd ch of turning ch-3; ch 3 (counts as first hdc and ch-1 sp on following rows), turn.

Row 4: Sc in next dc; * ch 4, in next ch-3 lp work (sc, ch 3, sc); ch 4, sk next dc, in next dc work (sc, ch 3, sc); rep from * across to last dc; sc in last dc, ch 1, hdc in 3rd ch of turning ch-3; ch 4, turn.

Row 5: Dc in first hdc, ch 2, dc in next ch-1 sp; * ch 1, in next ch-3 lp work (sc, ch 3, sc); ch 1, in next ch-3 lp work (dc, ch 2) 3 times; dc in same lp; rep from * across to turning ch lp; ch 1, dc in lp, ch 2, in 2nd ch of turning ch-3 work (dc, ch 1, dc); ch 3, turn.

Row 6: Sc in next ch-1 sp; * ch 1, in next ch-3 lp work (CL, ch 2) 3 times; CL in same lp; ch 1, sk next ch-2 sp, in next ch-2 sp work (sc, ch 3, sc); rep from * across to turning ch lp; sc in lp, ch 1, hdc in 3rd ch of turning ch-4; ch 3, turn.

Rep Rows 3 through 6 for pattern.

10 + 5 chs

#80

Multiple of 10 + 5

> **PATTERN STITCH**
>
> **Popcorn** (PC): 5 dc in next sc, drop lp from hook, insert hook in first dc, draw dropped lp through, ch 1: PC made.

Row 1: In 5th ch from hook work (dc, ch 1) 3 times; sk next 3 chs, sc in next 3 chs, ch 1, sk next 3 chs; * in next ch work (dc, ch 1) 7 times; sk next 3 chs, sc in next 3 chs, ch 1, sk next 3 chs; rep from * across to last ch; in last ch work (dc, ch 1) 3 times; dc in same ch; ch 1, turn.

Row 2 (right side): (Sc in next dc and in next ch-1 sp) twice; ch 1, sk next sc, in next sc work [PC (see Pattern Stitch), ch 3, PC]: PC shell made; * ch 1, sk next 2 ch-1 sps, (sc in next ch-1 sp and in next dc) 3 times; sc in next ch-1 sp, ch 1, sk next sc, in next sc work (PC, ch 3, PC): PC shell made; rep from * across to last 3 ch-1 sps; ch 1, sk next 2 ch-1 sps, sc in next ch-1 sp, in next dc, and in next 2 chs of beg 4 skipped chs; ch 1, turn.

Row 3: Sc in next 2 sc; * ch 1, in next ch-3 lp work (dc, ch 1) 7 times; sk next 2 sc, sc in next 3 sc; rep from * across to last 4 sc; ch 1, sk next 2 sc, sc in last 2 sc; ch 4, turn.

Row 4: PC in first sc; * ch 1, sk next 2 ch-1 sps, (sc in next ch-1 sp and in next dc) 3 times; sc in next ch-1 sp, ch 1, sk next sc, PC shell in next sc; rep from * across to last 2 sc; ch 1, sk next sc, in last sc work (PC, ch 1, dc); ch 4, turn.

Row 5: In next ch-1 sp work (dc, ch 1) 3 times; * sk next 2 sc, sc in next 3 sc, ch 1, in next ch-3 lp work (dc, ch 1) 7 times; rep from * across to last PC; ch 1, sk last PC, in 3rd ch of turning ch-4 work (dc, ch 1) 3 times; dc in same ch; ch 1, turn.

Row 6: (Sc in next dc and in next ch-1 sp) twice; ch 1, sk next sc, PC shell in next sc; * ch 1, sk next 2 ch-1 sps, (sc in next ch-1 sp and in next dc) 3 times; sc in next ch-1 sp, ch 1, sk next sc, PC shell in next sc; rep from * across to last 3 ch-1 sps; ch 1, sk next 2 ch-1 sps, sc in next ch-1 sp, in next dc, and in next 2 chs of turning ch-4; ch 1, turn.

Rep Rows 3 through 6 for pattern.

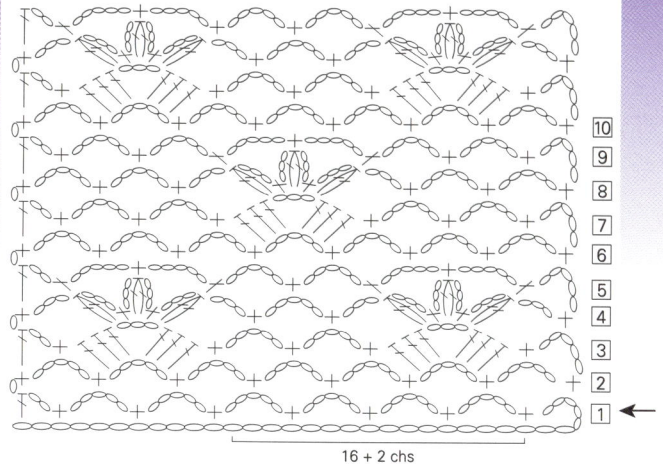

16 + 2 chs

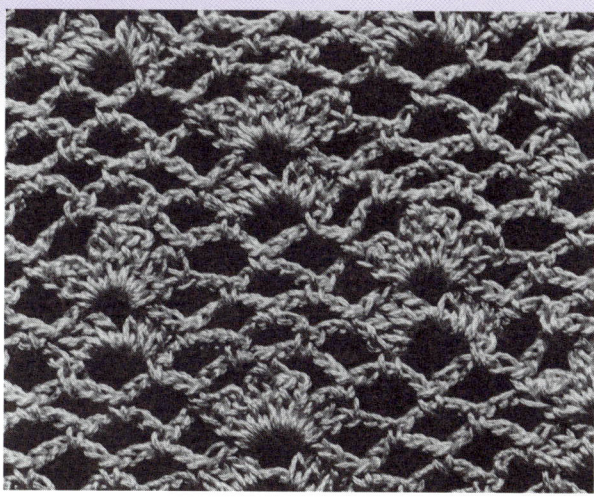

#81

Multiple 16 + 2

PATTERN STITCH

Cluster (CL): Keeping last lp of each dc on hook, 2 dc in next lp, YO and draw through all 3 lps on hook: CL made.

Row 1 (right side): Sc in 8th ch from hook; * ch 5, sk next 3 chs, sc in next ch; rep from * across to last 2 chs; ch 2, sk next ch, dc in last ch; ch 1, turn.

Row 2: Sc in next dc; * ch 5, sc in next ch-5 lp; rep from * across to beg 7 skipped chs; sc in 5th ch of 7 skipped chs; ch 5, turn.

Row 3: * Sc in next ch-5 lp, in next ch-5 lp work (3 dc, ch 3, 3 dc); (sc in next ch-5 lp, ch 5) twice; rep from * across to last ch-5 lp; sc in last ch-5 lp, ch 2, dc in last sc; ch 1, turn.

Row 4: Sc in next dc; * ch 3, in next ch-3 lp work [CL (see Pattern Stitch), ch 3, sc, ch 3] twice; CL in same lp; ch 3, sc in next ch-5 lp, ch 5, sc in next ch-5 lp; rep from * across to turning ch; ch 3, sc in 3rd ch of turning ch-5; ch 5, turn.

Row 5: * (Sc in next CL, ch 5) twice; sc in next CL, ch 5, sc in next ch-5 lp, ch 5; rep from * across to last ch-3 lp; sc in last ch-3 lp, ch 2, dc in last sc; ch 1, turn.

Row 6: Sc in next dc; * ch 5, sc in next ch-5 lp; rep from * across to turning ch; sc in 3rd ch of turning ch-5; ch 5, turn.

Row 7: * (Sc in next ch-5 lp, ch 5) twice; sc in next ch-5 lp, in next ch-5 lp work (3 dc, ch 3, 3 dc); rep from * across to last sc; ch 2, dc in last sc; ch 1, turn.

Row 8: Sc in next dc, (ch 5, sc in next ch-5 lp) twice; * ch 3, in next ch-3 lp work (CL, ch 3, sc, ch 3) twice; CL in same lp; ch 3, (sc in next ch-5 lp, ch 5) twice; sc in next ch-5 lp; rep from * across to turning ch; sc in 3rd ch of turning ch-5; ch 5, turn.

Row 9: (Sc in next ch-5 lp, ch 5) twice; * (sc in next CL, ch 5) twice; sc in next CL; ch 5, sc in next ch-5 lp, ch 5; rep from * across to last ch-5 lp, sc in last ch-5 lp, ch 2, dc in last sc; ch 1, turn.

Row 10: Sc in next dc; * ch 5, sc in next ch-5 lp; rep from * across to turning ch; sc in 3rd ch of turning ch-5; ch 5, turn.

Rep Rows 3 through 10 for pattern.

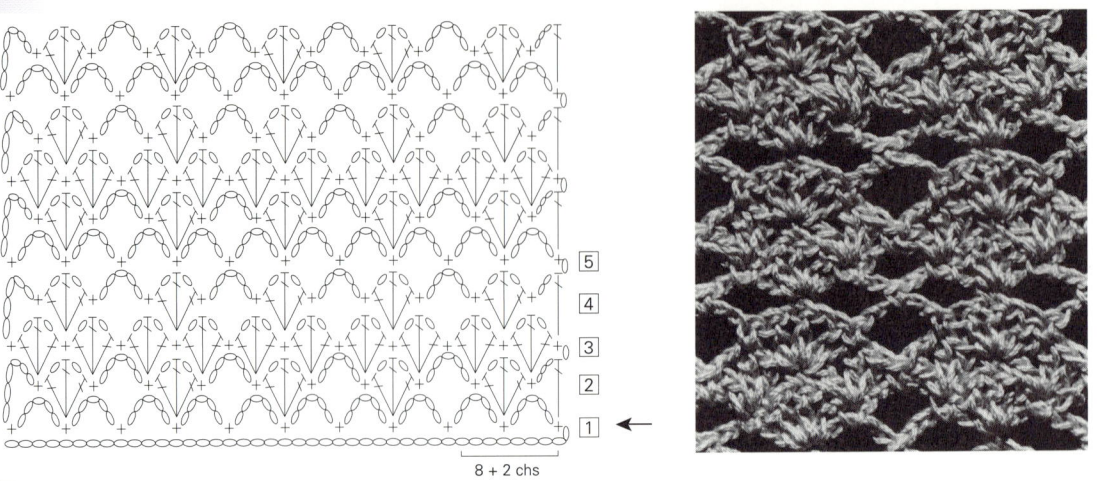

8 + 2 chs

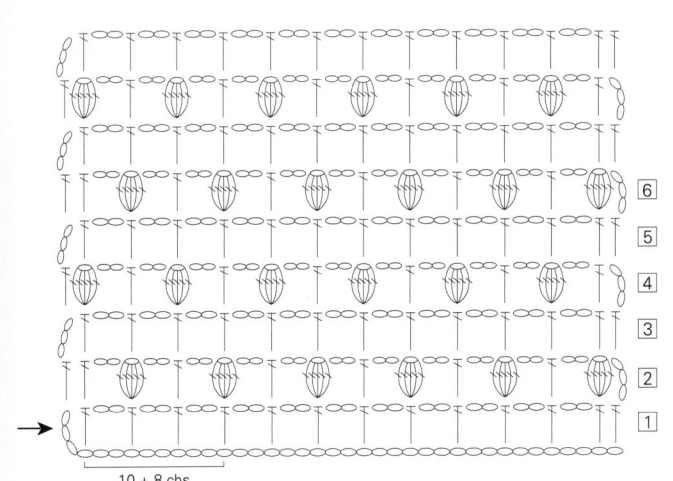 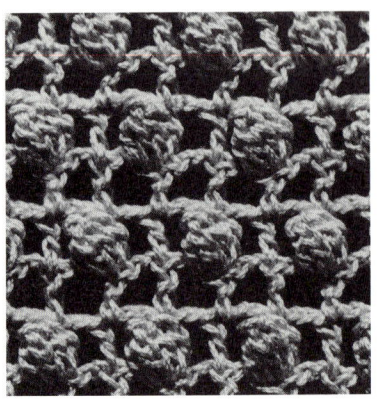

10 + 8 chs

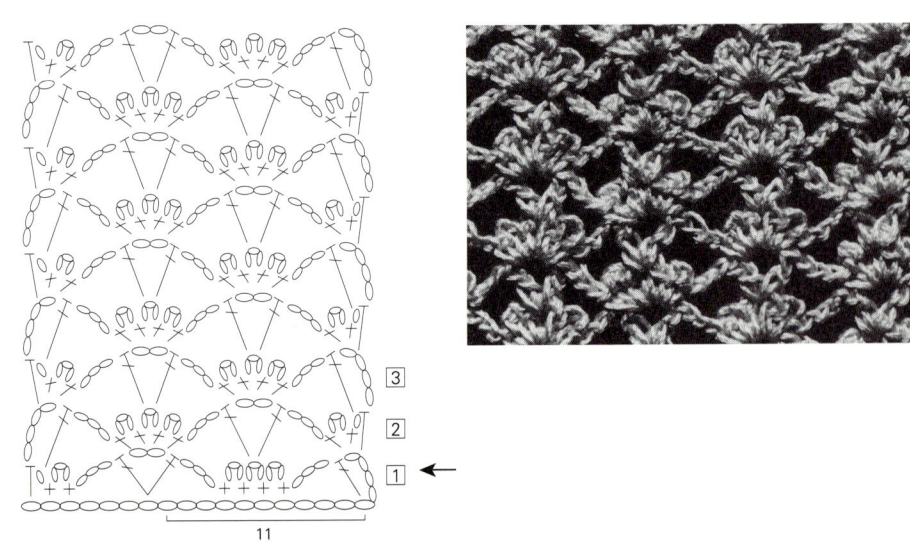

11

#82

Multiple of 8 + 2

Row 1 (right side): Sc in 2nd ch from hook; * ch 5, sk next 3 chs, sc in next ch; rep from * across; ch 6, turn.

Row 2: Sc in next lp; * in next sc work (dc, ch 1, dc, ch 1, dc); sc in next ch-5 lp, ch 5, sc in next ch-5 lp; rep from * across to last sc; ch 3, dc in last sc; ch 1, turn.

Row 3: Sc in next dc; * in next sc work (dc, ch 1, dc, ch 1, dc); sk next dc, sc in next dc, in next sc work (dc, ch 1, dc, ch 1, dc); sc in next ch-5 lp; rep from * across to turning ch lp; sc in lp; ch 5, turn.

Row 4: Sk next dc, sc in next dc, in next sc work (dc, ch 1, dc, ch 1, dc); sk next dc, sc in next dc; * ch 5, sk next dc, next sc, and next dc, sc in next dc, in next sc work (dc, ch 1, dc, ch 1, dc); sk next dc, sc in next dc; rep from * across to last sc; ch 2, dc in last sc; ch 1, turn.

Row 5: Sc in next dc, ch 5, sk next dc, sc in next dc; * ch 5, sc in next ch-5 lp, ch 5, sk next dc, sc in next dc; rep from * across to turning ch lp; ch 5, sc in lp; ch 6, turn.

Rep Rows 2 through 5 for pattern.

#83

Multiple of 10 + 8

> **PATTERN STITCH**
>
> **Popcorn** (PC): 5 dc in next dc, drop lp from hook, insert lp from back to front in first dc, draw dropped lp through, ch 1: PC made.

Row 1: Dc in 4th ch from hook; * ch 2, sk next 2 chs, dc in next ch; rep from * across to last ch; dc in last ch; ch 3 (counts as first dc on following rows), turn.

Row 2 (right side): PC (see Pattern Stitch) in next dc; ch 2, dc in next dc; * ch 2, PC in next dc; ch 2, dc in next dc; rep from * across to beg 3 skipped chs; dc in 3rd ch of 3 skipped chs; ch 3, turn.

Row 3: Dc in next dc, ch 2, dc in top of next PC; * ch 2, dc in next dc, ch 2, dc in top of next PC; rep from * across to turning ch; dc in 3rd ch of turning ch-3; ch 3, turn.

Row 4: Dc in next dc, ch 2, PC in next dc; * ch 2, dc in next dc, ch 2, PC in next dc; rep from * across to turning ch; dc in 3rd ch of turning ch-3; ch 3, turn.

Row 5: Dc in top of next PC, ch 2, dc in next dc; * ch 2, dc in top of next PC, ch 2, dc in next dc; rep from * across to turning ch; dc in 3rd ch of turning ch-3; ch 3, turn.

Row 6: PC in next dc; ch 2, dc in next dc; * ch 2, PC in next dc; ch 2, dc in next dc; rep from * across to turning ch; dc in 3rd ch of turning ch-3; ch 3, turn.

Rep Rows 3 through 6 for pattern.

#84

Multiple of 11

Row 1 (right side): Dc in 5th ch from hook; * ch 3, sk next 3 chs, (sc in next ch, ch 3) 3 times; sc in next ch, ch 3, sk next 3 chs, in next ch work (dc, ch 2, dc); rep from * across to last 6 chs; ch 3, sk next 3 chs, sc in next ch, ch 3, sc in next ch, ch 1, hdc in last ch; ch 4, turn.

Row 2: Dc in next ch-1 sp; * ch 3, in next ch-2 sp work (sc, ch 3) 4 times; sk next 2 ch-3 lps, in next ch-3 lp work (dc, ch 2, dc); rep from * across to lp formed by beg 4 skipped chs; ch 3, in lp work (sc, ch 3, sc, ch 1, hdc); ch 4, turn.

Row 3: Dc in next ch-1 sp; * ch 3, in next ch-2 sp work (sc, ch 3) 4 times; sk next 2 ch-3 lps, in next ch-3 lp work (dc, ch 2, dc); rep from * across to turning ch lp; ch 3, in lp work (sc, ch 3, sc, ch 1, hdc); ch 4, turn.

Rep Row 3 for pattern.

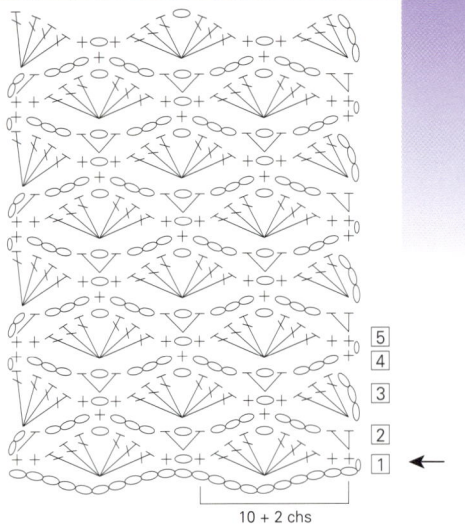

#85

Multiple of 10 + 2

Row 1 (right side): Sc in 2nd and 3rd chs from hook; * sk next 3 chs, in next ch work (3 dc, ch 1, 3 dc); sk next 3 chs, sc in next ch, ch 1, sk next ch, sc in next ch; rep from * across to last ch; sc in last ch; ch 2, turn.

Row 2: Hdc in first sc; * ch 3, sc in next ch-1 sp, ch 3, in next ch-1 sp work (hdc, ch 1, hdc); rep from * across to last 2 sc; sk next sc, 2 hdc in last sc; ch 3, turn.

Row 3: 3 dc in first hdc; * sk next 2 chs, sc in next ch, ch 1, sk next sc, sc in next ch, sk next 2 chs, in next ch-1 sp work (3 dc, ch 1, 3 dc); rep from * across to turning ch; 4 dc in 2nd ch of turning ch-2; ch 1, turn.

Row 4: Sc in next dc; * ch 3, in next ch-1 sp work (hdc, ch 1, hdc); ch 3, sc in next ch-1 sp; rep from * across to turning ch; sc in 3rd ch of turning ch-3; ch 1, turn.

Row 5: Sc in next sc and in next ch; * in next ch-1 sp work (3 dc, ch 1, 3 dc); sk next 2 chs, sc in next ch, ch 1, sk next sc, sc in next ch; rep from * across to last sc; sc in last sc; ch 2, turn.

Rep Rows 2 through 5 for pattern.

25 + 15 chs

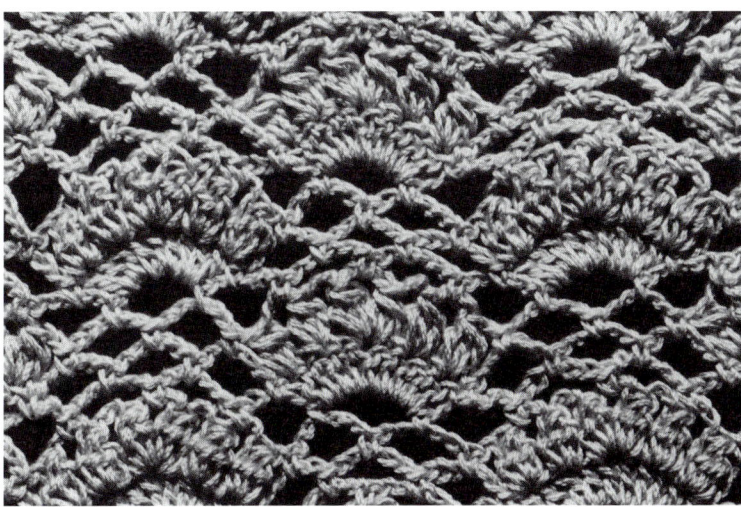

#86

Multiple of 25 + 15

PATTERN STITCH

Cluster (CL): Keeping last lp of each dc on hook, 3 dc in next st, YO and draw through all 4 lps on hook: CL made.

Row 1 (right side): Sc in 2nd ch from hook; * ch 5, sk next 4 chs, sc in next ch; rep from * across to last 3 chs; ch 2, sk next 2 chs, dc in last ch; ch 3, turn.

Row 2: 4 dc in next ch-2 sp; * (sc in next ch-5 lp, ch 5) 3 times; sc in next ch-5 lp, 9 dc in next ch-5 lp; rep from * across to last 2 ch-5 lps; sc in next ch-5 lp, ch 5, sc in last ch-5 lp, ch 2, dc in last sc; ch 1, turn.

Row 3: Sc in next dc, ch 5; * sc in next ch-5 lp, ch 1, [CL (see Pattern Stitch) in next dc, ch 3, sk next dc] twice; in next dc work (CL, ch 3, CL); (ch 3, sk next dc, CL in next dc) twice; ch 1, (sc in next ch-5 lp, ch 5) twice; rep from * across to last ch-5 lp; sc in last ch-5 lp, ch 1, (CL in next dc, ch 3, sk next dc) twice; in 3rd ch of turning ch-3 work (CL, ch 1, trc); ch 1, turn.

Row 4: Sc in next trc, ch 5, sk next ch-3 lp, sc in next ch-3 lp; * (ch 5, sc in next ch-5 lp) twice; ch 5, sc in next ch-3 lp, (ch 5, sk next ch-3 lp, sc in next ch-3 lp) twice; rep from * across to last ch-5 lp; ch 5, sc in last ch-5 lp, ch 2, dc in last sc; ch 3, turn.

Row 5: 4 dc in next ch-2 sp; * (sc in next ch-5 lp, ch 5) 3 times; sc in next ch-5 lp, 9 dc in next ch-5 lp; rep from * across to last 2 ch-5 lps; sc in next ch-5 lp, ch 5, sc in last ch-5 lp, ch 2, dc in last sc; ch 1, turn.

Row 6: Sc in next dc, ch 5; * sc in next ch-5 lp, ch 1, (CL in next dc, ch 3, sk next dc) twice; in next dc work (CL, ch 3, CL); (ch 3, sk next dc, CL in next dc) twice; ch 1, (sc in next ch-5 lp, ch 5) twice; rep from * across to last ch-5 lp; sc in last ch-5 lp, ch 1, (CL in next dc, ch 3, sk next dc) twice; in 3rd ch of turning ch-3 work (CL, ch 1, trc); ch 1, turn.

Row 7: Rep Row 4.

Rep Rows 2 through 7 for pattern.

7 + 3 chs

#87

Multiple of 7 + 3

Row 1: Sc in 2nd ch from hook, ch 1, sk next ch; * sc in next ch, ch 5, sk next 3 chs, sc in next ch, ch 3, sk next 2 chs; rep from * across to last 7 chs; sc in next ch, ch 5, sk next 3 chs, sc in next ch, ch 1, sk next ch, sc in last ch; ch 1, turn.

Row 2 (right side): Sc in next sc; * 7 dc in next ch-5 lp; sc in next ch-3 lp; rep from * across to last ch-5 lp; 7 dc in last ch-5 lp; sk next sc, sc in last sc; ch 5 (counts as first dc and a ch-2 sp on following rows), turn.

Row 3: Sk next 2 dc; * sc in next 3 dc, ch 5, sk next 5 sts; rep from * across to last 6 sts; sc in next 3 dc, ch 2, sk next 2 dc, dc in last sc; ch 1, turn.

Row 4: Sc in next dc; * ch 3, sk next sc, 2 dc in next sc; ch 3, sc in next ch-5 lp; rep from * across to last 3 sc; ch 3, sk next sc, 2 dc in next sc; ch 3, sc in 3rd ch of turning ch-5; ch 5, turn.

Row 5: * Sc in next ch-3 lp, ch 3, sc in next ch-3 lp, ch 5; rep from * across to last 2 ch-3 lps; sc in next ch-3 lp, ch 3, sc in last ch-3 lp, ch 2, dc in last sc; ch 3, turn.

Row 6: 3 dc in next ch-2 sp; * sc in next ch-3 lp, 7 dc in next ch-5 lp; rep from * across to last ch-3 lp; sc in last ch-3 lp, 3 dc in turning ch lp; dc in 3rd ch of turning ch-5; ch 1, turn.

Row 7: Sc in next 2 dc; * ch 5, sk next 5 sts, sc in next 3 dc; rep from * across to last 6 sts; ch 5, sk next 5 sts, sc in last dc and in 3rd ch of turning ch-3; ch 3, turn.

Row 8: Dc in first sc; * ch 3, sc in next ch-5 lp, ch 3, sk next sc, 2 dc in next sc; rep from * across; ch 1, turn.

Row 9: Sc in next dc, ch 1; * sc in next ch-3 lp, ch 5, sc in next ch-3 lp, ch 3; rep from * across to last 2 ch-3 lps; sc in next ch-3 lp, ch 5, sc in last ch-3 lp, ch 1, sk next dc, sc in 3rd ch of turning ch-3; ch 1, turn.

Rep Rows 2 through 9 for pattern.

12 + 10 chs

#88

Multiple of 12 + 10

Row 1 (right side): Sc in 6th ch from hook; * ch 3, sk next 2 chs, sc in next ch; rep from * across to last ch; ch 1, dc in last ch; ch 1, turn.

Row 2: Sc in next dc, ch 3, sc in next ch-3 lp; * 5 dc in next ch-3 lp; sc in next ch-3 lp, (ch 3, sc in next ch-3 lp) twice; rep from * across to lp formed by beg 5 skipped chs; 3 dc in lp; ch 3, turn.

Row 3: Dc in first dc, 2 dc in each of next 2 dc; * ch 1, sc in next ch-3 lp, ch 3, sc in next ch-3 lp, ch 1, 2 dc in each of next 5 dc; rep from * across to last ch-3 lp; ch 1, sc in last ch-3 lp, ch 1, dc in last sc; ch 4, turn.

Row 4: Dc in next ch-1 sp, ch 1, sc between next two 2-dc groups; * (ch 3, sc between next two 2-dc groups) 3 times; ch 1, in next ch-3 lp work (dc, ch 3, dc); ch 1, sc between next two 2-dc groups; rep from * across to last two 2-dc groups; ch 1, sc between next 2-dc groups, ch 3, sc between next 2-dc group and last dc, ch 3, sc in 3rd ch of turning ch-3; ch 2, turn.

Row 5: Sc in next ch-3 lp, ch 3, sc in next ch-3 lp; * 5 dc in next ch-3 lp; sc in next ch-3 lp, (ch 3, sc in next ch-3 lp) twice; rep from * across to turning ch lp; 3 dc in lp; ch 3, turn.

Rep Rows 3 through 5 for pattern.

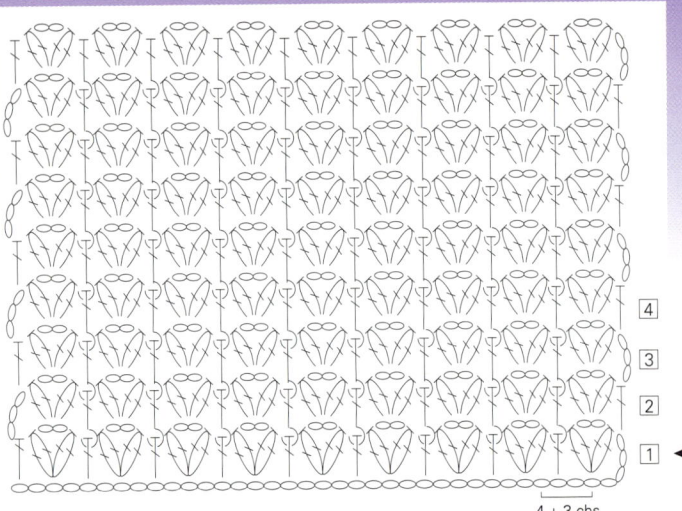

#89

Multiple of 4 + 3

PATTERN STITCHES

Cluster (CL): Keeping last lp of each dc on hook, 2 dc in next st, YO and draw through all 3 lps on hook: CL made.

Front Post Double Crochet (FPdc): YO, insert hook from front to back to front around post (see page 8) of next dc; YO and draw lp through, (YO and draw through 2 lps on hook) twice: FPdc made.

Back Post Double Crochet (BPdc): YO, insert hook from back to front to back around post (see page 8) of next dc; YO and draw lp through, (YO and draw through 2 lps on hook) twice: BPdc made.

Row 1 (right side): In 5th ch from hook work [CL (see Pattern Stitches), ch 2, CL]; * sk next ch, dc in next ch, sk next ch, in next ch work (CL, ch 2, CL); rep from * across to last 2 chs; sk next ch, dc in last ch; ch 3, turn.

Row 2: * In next ch-2 sp work (CL, ch 2, CL); BPdc (see Pattern Stitches) around next dc; rep from * across to last ch-2 sp; in last ch-2 sp work (CL, ch 2, CL); dc in 4th ch of beg 4 skipped chs; ch 3, turn.

Row 3: * In next ch-2 sp work (CL, ch 2, CL); FPdc (see Pattern Stitches) around next BPdc; rep from * across to last ch-2 sp; in last ch-2 sp work (CL, ch 2, CL); dc in 3rd ch of turning ch-3; ch 3, turn.

Row 4: * In next ch-2 sp work (CL, ch 2, CL); BPdc around next FPdc; rep from * across to last ch-2 sp; in last ch-2 sp work (CL, ch 2, CL); dc in 3rd ch of turning ch-3; ch 3, turn.

Rep Rows 3 and 4 for pattern.

Multiple of 9 + 2

> **PATTERN STITCH**
>
> **Popcorn** (PC): 4 dc in next sp, drop lp from hook, insert hook in first dc, draw dropped lp through, ch 1: PC made.

Row 1 (right side): Sc in 2nd ch from hook and in each rem ch across; ch 3, turn.

Row 2: Sk first 3 sc, sc in next sc, ch 4, sk next 2 sc, sc in next sc, ch 3, sk next 2 sc; * sc in next sc, ch 3, sk next 2 sc, sc in next sc, ch 4, sk next 2 sc, sc in next sc, ch 3, sk next 2 sc; rep from * across to last sc; sc in last sc; ch 3, turn.

Row 3: Sc in next ch-3 lp, ch 3, in next ch-4 lp work [PC (see Pattern Stitch, ch 2, PC, ch 2, PC]; * ch 3, (sc in next ch-3 lp, ch 3) twice; in next ch-4 lp work (PC, ch 2, PC, ch 2, PC); rep from * across to turning ch lp; ch 3, dc in lp; ch 3, turn.

Row 4: Sk next ch-3 lp, sc in next ch-2 sp, ch 4, sc in next ch-2 sp; * ch 3, sk next ch-3 lp, dc in next ch-3 lp, ch 3, sk next ch-3 lp, sc in next ch-2 sp, ch 4, sc in next ch-2 sp; rep from * across to turning ch lp; ch 3, dc in lp; ch 3, turn.

Rep Rows 3 and 4 for pattern.

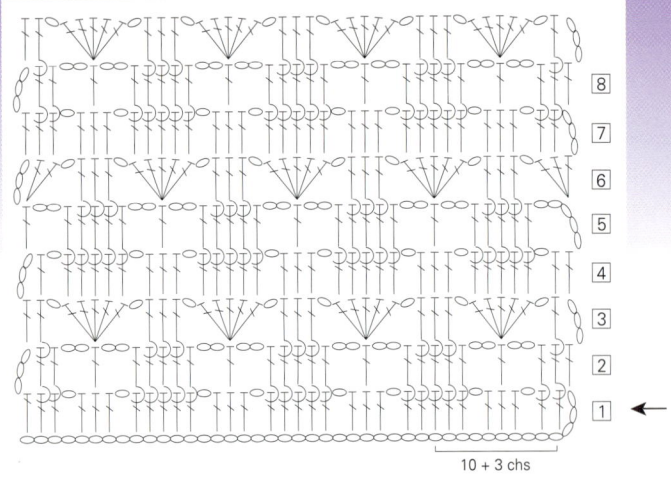

10 + 3 chs

#91

Multiple of 10 + 3

PATTERN STITCHES

Front Post Double Crochet (FPdc): YO, insert hook from front to back to front around post (see page 8) of next dc; YO and draw lp through, (YO and draw through 2 lps on hook) twice: FPdc made.

Back Post Double Crochet (BPdc): YO, insert hook from back to front to back around post (see page 8) of next dc; YO and draw lp through, (YO and draw through 2 lps on hook) twice: BPdc made.

Row 1 (right side): Dc in 4th and 5th chs from hook; * ch 1, sk next ch, dc in next 3 chs, ch 1, sk next ch, dc in next 5 chs; rep from * across to last 4 chs; ch 1, sk next ch, dc in last 3 chs; ch 3 (counts as first dc on following rows), turn.

Row 2: BPdc (see Pattern Stitches) around of each of next 2 dc; * ch 2, sk next dc, dc in next dc, ch 2, sk next dc, BPdc around each of next 5 dc; rep from * across to last 2 dc; ch 2, BPdc around each of next 2 dc; dc in 3rd ch of beg 3 skipped chs; ch 3, turn.

Row 3: FPdc (see Pattern Stitches) around next BPdc; * ch 1, sk next BPdc, 5 dc in next dc; ch 1, sk next BPdc, FPdc around each of next 3 BPdc; rep from * across to turning ch; dc in 3rd ch of turning ch-3; ch 3, turn.

Row 4: Dc in next FPdc; * ch 1, dc in next 5 dc, ch 1, dc in next 3 FPdc; rep from * across to turning ch; dc in 3rd ch of turning ch-3; ch 5, turn.

Row 5: * Sk next dc and next ch-1 sp, FPdc around each of next 5 dc; ch 2, sk next dc, dc in next dc, ch 2; rep from * across to last ch-1 sp; ch 2, sk last ch-1 sp and next dc, dc in 3rd ch of turning ch-3; ch 3, turn.

Row 6: 2 dc in first dc; * ch 1, sk next FPdc; BPdc around each of next 3 FPdc; ch 1, sk next ch-2 sp, 5 dc in next dc; rep from * across to turning ch; ch 1, 3 dc in 3rd ch of turning ch-5; ch 3, turn.

Row 7: Dc in next 2 dc; * ch 1, dc in next 3 BPdc, ch 1, dc in next 5 dc; rep from * across to turning ch; dc in 3rd ch of turning ch-3; ch 3, turn.

Row 8: BPdc around of each of next 2 dc; * ch 2, sk next dc, dc in next dc, ch 2, sk next dc, BPdc around each of next 5 dc; rep from * across to turning ch; dc in 3rd ch of turning ch-3; ch 3, turn.

Rep Rows 3 through 8 for pattern.

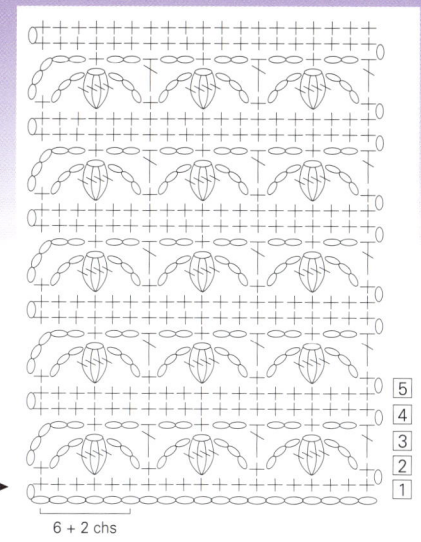

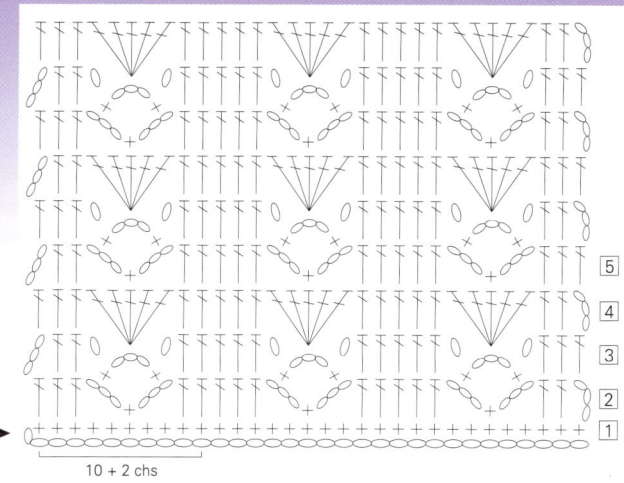

#92

Multiple of 6 + 2

PATTERN STITCH

Popcorn (PC): 4 dc in next sc, drop lp from hook, insert hook in first dc, draw dropped lp through, ch 1: PC made.

Row 1: Sc in 2nd ch from hook and in each rem ch; ch 1, turn.

Row 2 (right side): Sc in next sc; * ch 3, sk next 2 sc, PC (see Pattern Stitch) in next sc; ch 3, sk next 2 sc, sc in next sc; rep from * across; ch 5, turn.

Row 3: Sc in next PC, ch 2, dc in next sc; * ch 2, sc in next PC, ch 2, dc in next sc; rep from * across; ch 1, turn.

Row 4: Sc in each st and in each ch across to turning ch; sc in next 3 chs of turning ch-5; ch 1, turn.

Row 5: Sc in each sc; ch 1, turn.

Rep Rows 2 through 5 for pattern.

#93

Multiple of 10 + 2

Row 1: Sc in 2nd ch from hook and in each rem ch; ch 3 (counts as first dc on following rows), turn.

Row 2 (right side): Dc in next 2 sc; * ch 3, sk next 2 sc, sc in next sc, ch 3, sk next 2 sc, dc in next 5 sc; rep from * across to last 3 sc; dc in last 3 sc; ch 3, turn.

Row 3: Dc in next 2 dc; * ch 1, sc in next ch-3 lp, ch 3, sc in next ch-3 lp, ch 1, dc in next 5 dc; rep from * across to last 2 dc; dc in last 2 dc and in 3rd ch of turning ch-3; ch 3, turn.

Row 4: Dc in next 2 dc; * 5 dc in next ch-3 lp; dc in next 5 dc; rep from * across to last 2 dc; dc in last 2 dc and in 3rd ch of turning ch-3; ch 3, turn.

Row 5: Dc in next 2 dc; * ch 3, sk next 2 dc, sc in next dc, ch 3, sk next 2 dc, dc in next 5 dc; rep from * across to last 2 dc; dc in last 2 dc and in 3rd ch of turning ch-3; ch 3, turn.

Rep Rows 3 through 5 for pattern.

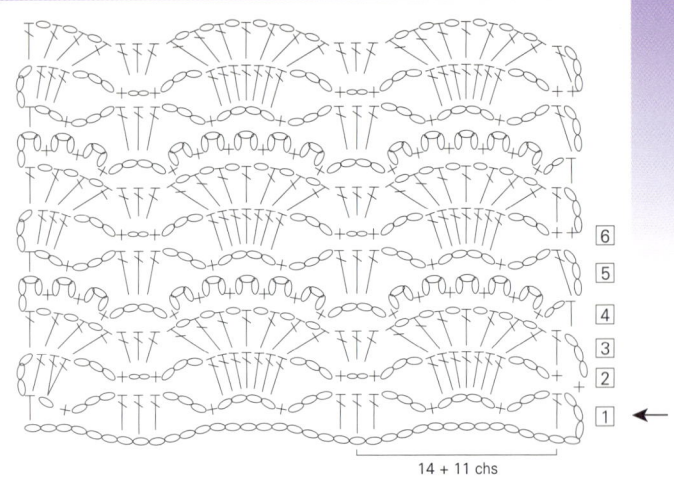

14 + 11 chs

#94

Multiple of 14 + 11

Row 1 (right side): Dc in 5th ch from hook; * ch 3, sk next 3 chs, sc in next ch, ch 4, sk next 3 chs, sc in next ch, ch 3, sk next 3 chs, dc in next 3 chs; rep from * across to last 6 chs; ch 3, sk next 3 chs, sc in next ch, ch 1, sk next ch, hdc in last ch; ch 3 (counts as first dc on following rows), turn.

Row 2: Dc in first hdc, 2 dc in next ch-1 sp; * ch 3, sc in next dc, ch 2, sk next dc, sc in next dc, ch 3, sk next ch-3 lp, 7 dc in next ch-4 lp; rep from * across to last dc; ch 3, sc in last dc, sc in 3rd ch of beg 4 skipped chs; ch 3, turn.

Row 3: Dc in next sc; * (dc in next dc, ch 1) 6 times; dc in next dc, sk next ch-3 lp, 3 dc in next ch-2 sp; rep from * across to last 3 dc; (dc in next dc, ch 1) 3 times; dc in 3rd ch of turning ch-3; ch 4, turn.

Row 4: (Sc in next ch-1 sp, ch 3) twice; * sc in next ch-1 sp, ch 4, sk next 5 dc, (sc in next ch-1 sp, ch 3) 5 times; rep from * across to last ch-1 sp; sc in last ch-1 sp, ch 2, hdc in 3rd ch of turning ch-3; ch 3, turn.

Row 5: Dc in first hdc, ch 3, sk next ch-2 sp and next ch-3 lp; * sc in next ch-3 lp, ch 4, sk next ch-3 lp, sc in next ch-3 lp, ch 3, sk next ch-3 lp, 3 dc in next ch-4 lp; ch 3, sk next ch-3 lp; rep from * across to last ch-3 lp; ch 3, sc in last ch-3 lp, ch 2, hdc in 3rd ch of turning ch-4; ch 3, turn.

Row 6: 3 dc in next ch-2 sp; * ch 3, sk next ch-3 lp, sc in next dc, ch 2, sk next dc, sc in next dc, ch 3, sk next ch-3 lp, 7 dc in next ch-4 lp; rep from * across to turning ch; sc in 3rd ch of turning ch-3; ch 3, turn.

Rep Rows 3 through 6 for pattern.

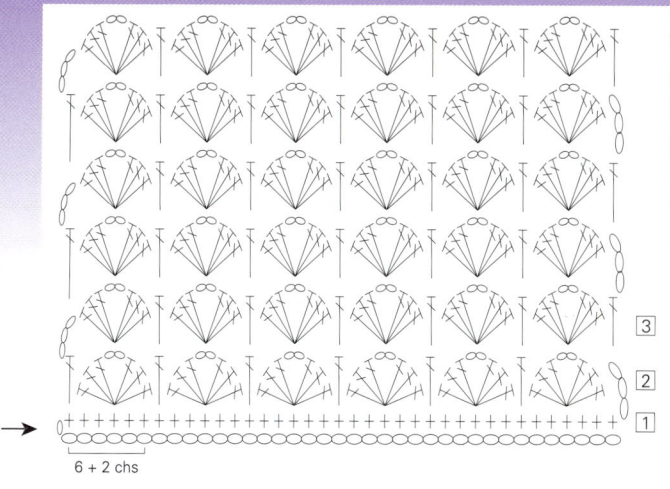

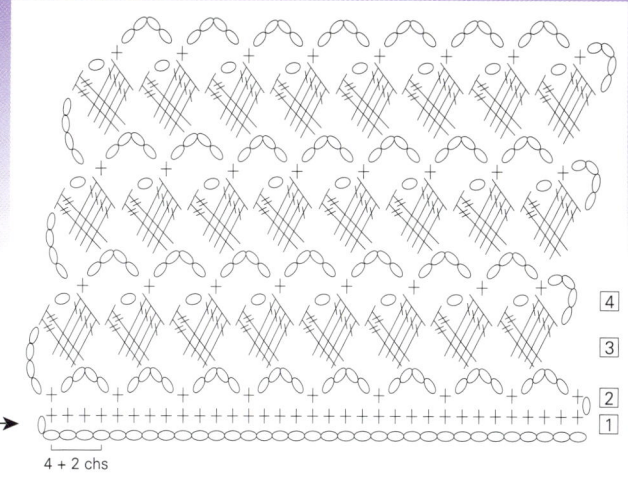

#95

Multiple of 6 + 2

Row 1: Sc in 2nd ch from hook and in each rem ch; ch 3 (counts as first dc on following rows), turn.

Row 2 (right side): * Sk next 2 sc, in next sc work (3 dc, ch 2, 3 dc): shell made; sk next 2 sc, dc in next sc; rep from * across; ch 3, turn.

Row 3: * Shell in ch-2 sp of next shell; dc in next dc; rep from * across to turning ch; dc in 3rd ch of turning ch-3; ch 3, turn.

Rep Row 3 for pattern.

#96

Multiple of 4 + 2

Row 1: Sc in 2nd ch from hook and in each rem ch; ch 1, turn.

Row 2 (right side): Sc in next sc; * ch 4, sk next 3 sc, sc in next sc; rep from * across; ch 4, turn.

Row 3: * 2 trc in next ch-4 lp; ch 1, 4 dc over side of 2 trc just made; rep from * across; ch 4, turn.

Row 4: Sk next 3 dc, sc in next dc; * ch 4, sk next 3 dc, sc in next dc; rep from * across; ch 4, turn.

Rep Rows 3 and 4 for pattern.

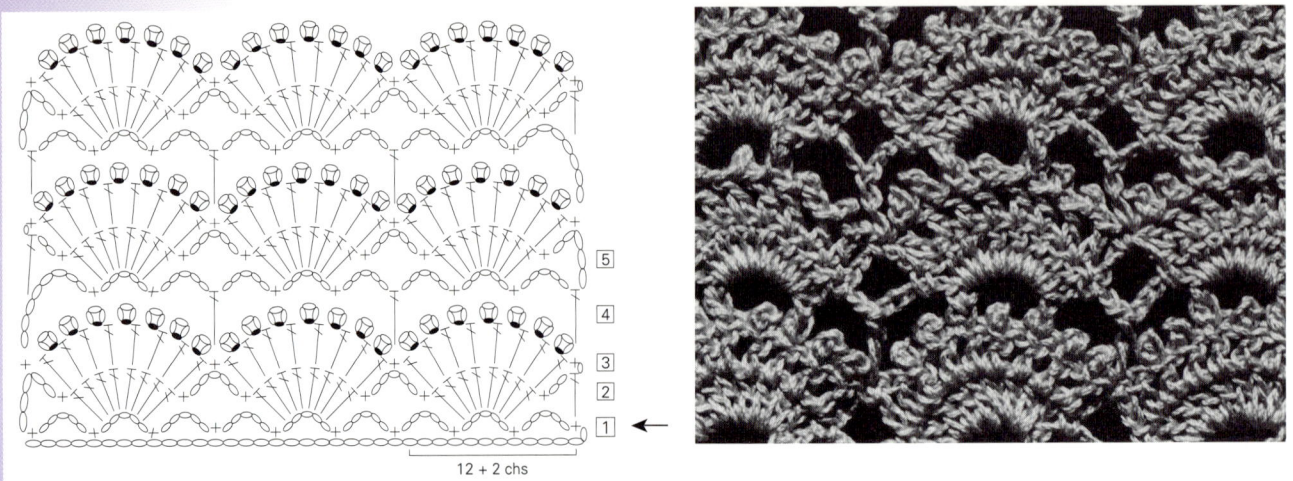

12 + 2 chs

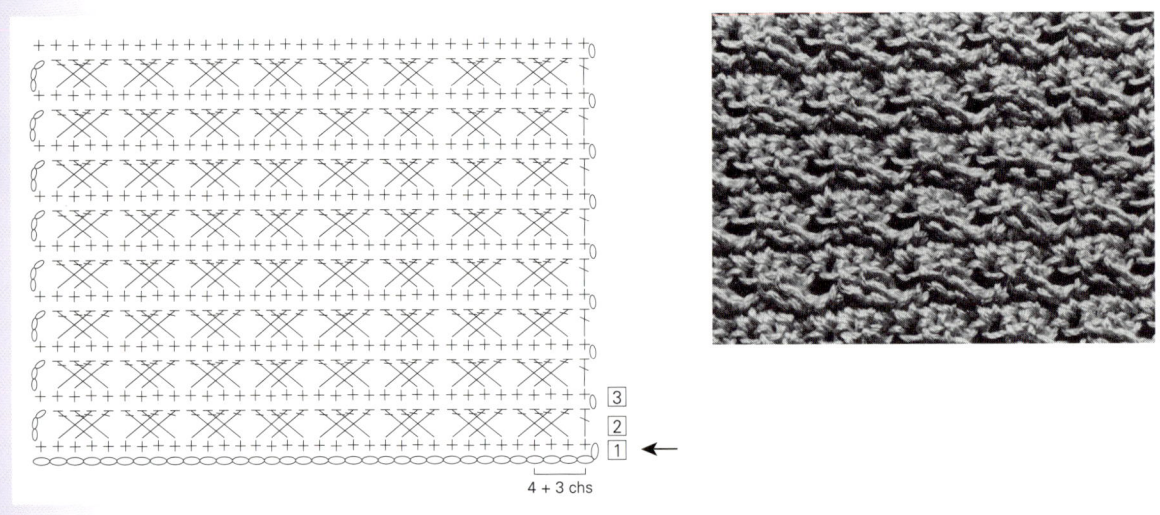

4 + 3 chs

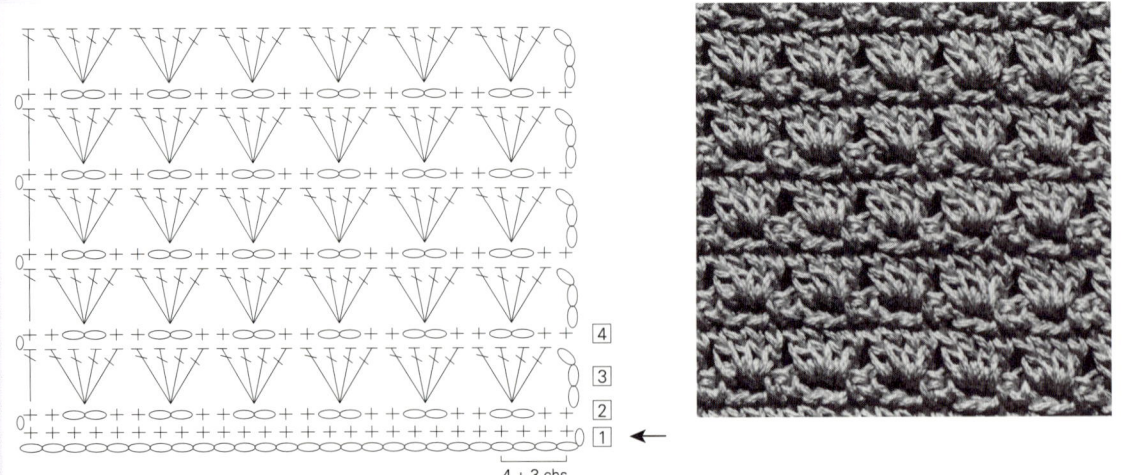

4 + 3 chs

#97

Multiple of 12 + 2

Row 1 (right side): Sc in 2nd ch from hook; * ch 5, sk next 3 chs, sc in next ch; rep from * across; ch 5, turn.

Row 2: Sc in next ch-5 lp; * 8 dc in next ch-5 lp; sc in next ch-5 lp, ch 5, sc in next ch-5 lp; rep from * across to last sc; ch 2, dc in last sc; ch 1, turn.

Row 3: Sc in next dc; * (dc in next dc, ch 3, sl st in dc just made: picot made) 7 times; dc in next dc, sc in next ch-5 lp; rep from * across to turning ch; sc in 3rd ch of turning ch-5; ch 8, turn.

Row 4: * Sk next 2 picots, sc in next picot, ch 5, sk next picot, sc in next picot, ch 5, sk next 2 picots, dc in next sc; rep from * across; ch 5, turn.

Row 5: Sc in next ch-5 lp; * 8 dc in next ch-5 lp; sc in next ch-5 lp, ch 5, sc in next ch-5 lp; rep from * across to turning ch lp; sc in lp, ch 2, dc in 3rd ch of turning ch-8; ch 1, turn.

Rep Rows 3 through 5 for pattern.

#98

Multiple of 4 + 3

Row 1 (right side): Sc in 2nd ch from hook and in each rem ch; ch 3 (counts as first dc on following rows), turn.

Row 2: Sk next 2 sc, dc in next 2 sc, dc in each skipped sc; * sk next 2 sc, dc in next 2 sc, dc in each skipped sc; rep from * across to last sc; dc in last sc; ch 1, turn.

Row 3: Sc in each dc to turning ch; sc in 3rd ch of turning ch-3; ch 3, turn.

Rep Rows 2 and 3 for pattern.

#99

Multiple of 4 + 3

Row 1 (right side): Sc in 2nd ch from hook and in each rem ch; ch 1, turn.

Row 2: Sc in next 2 sc; * ch 2, sk next 2 sc, sc in next 2 sc; rep from * across; ch 3, turn.

Row 3: 4 dc in each ch-2 sp across to last sc; dc in last sc; ch 1, turn.

Row 4: * Sc in next 2 dc, ch 2, sk next 2 dc; rep from * across to last 3 dc; ch 2, sk next 2 dc, sc in last dc and in 3rd ch of turning ch-3; ch 3, turn.

Rep Rows 3 and 4 for pattern.

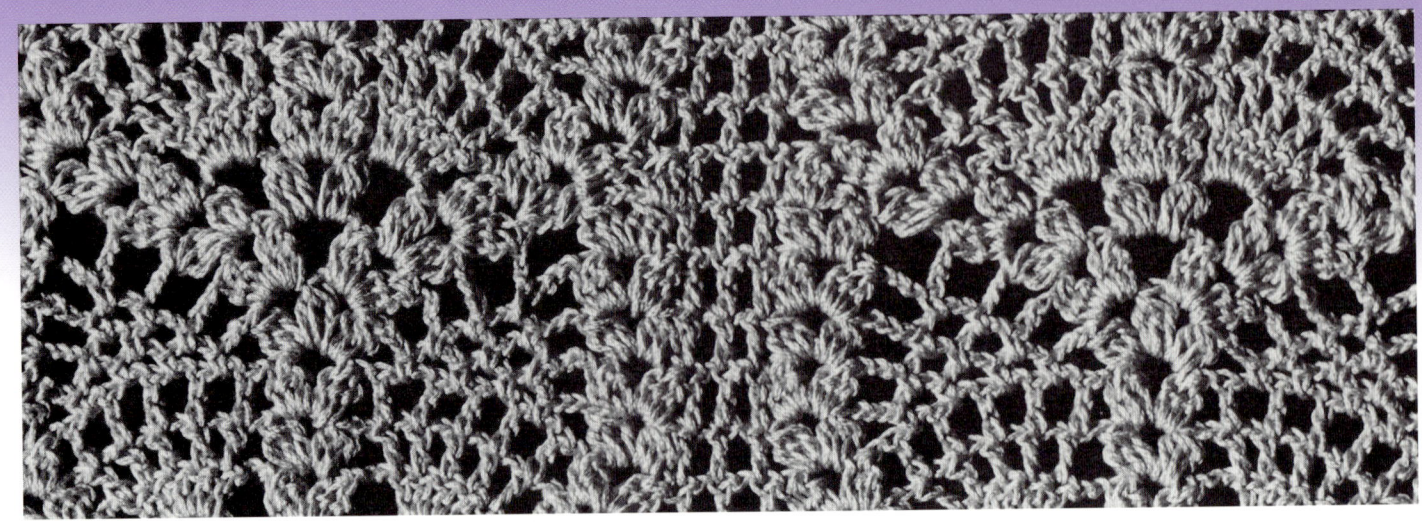

42 + 4 chs

#100

Multiple of 42 + 4

> **PATTERN STITCH**
>
> **Cluster** (CL): Keeping last lp of each dc on hook, 3 dc in next st or sp, YO, draw through all 4 lps on hook: CL made.

Row 1 (right side): Dc in 6th ch from hook, (ch 1, sk next ch, dc in next dc) 3 times; * sk next 2 chs, in next ch work [CL (see Pattern Stitch), ch 3, CL]: shell made; † ch 2, sk next 4 chs, in next ch work (dc, ch 4, dc); ch 2, sk next 4 chs, shell as before in next ch †; rep from † to † once more; sk next 2 chs, dc in next ch, (ch 1, sk next ch, dc in next ch) 8 times; rep from * across to last 11 chs; sk next 2 chs, dc in next ch, (ch 1, sk next ch, dc in next ch) 4 times; ch 4 (counts as first dc and ch-1 sp on following rows), turn.

Row 2: Dc in next dc, (ch 1, dc in next dc) twice; * shell in ch-3 lp of next shell: shell in shell made; ch 2, 5 dc in next ch-4 lp; ch 3, shell in next shell; ch 3, 5 dc in next ch-4 lp; ch 2, shell in next shell; sk next dc, dc in next dc, (ch 1, dc in next dc) 6 times; rep from * across to last 4 dc; sk next dc, dc in next dc, (ch 1, dc in next dc) twice; ch 1, dc in 4th ch of beg 5 skipped chs; ch 4, turn.

Row 3: Dc in next dc, ch 1, dc in next dc; * shell in next shell; † (ch 1, dc in next dc) 5 times; ch 1, shell in next shell †; rep from † to † once; sk next dc, dc in next dc, (ch 1, dc in next dc) 4 times; rep from * across to last 3 dc; sk next dc, dc in next dc, ch 1, dc in last dc, ch 1, dc in 3rd ch of turning ch-4; ch 4, turn.

Row 4: Dc in next dc; * shell in next shell; † ch 1, dc in next dc, (ch 2, dc in next dc) 4 times; ch 1, shell in next shell †; rep from † to † once more; sk next dc, dc in next dc, (ch 1, dc in next dc) twice; rep from * across to last 2 dc; sk next dc, dc in last dc; ch 1, dc in 3rd ch of turning ch-4; ch 4, turn.

Row 5: Dc in next dc; * shell in next shell; (ch 3, sc in next ch-2 sp) 4 times; ch 3, in next ch-3 lp work (CL, ch 3, CL, ch 3, CL); ch 3, (sc in next ch-2 sp, ch 3) 4 times; shell in next shell; dc in next dc, (ch 1, dc in next dc) twice; rep from * across to last dc; dc in last dc, ch 1, dc in 3rd ch of turning ch-4; ch 4, turn.

Row 6: Dc in next dc; * shell in next shell; ch 3, sk next ch-3 lp, (sc in next ch-3 lp, ch 3) 3 times; sk next ch-3 lp, shell in next ch-3 lp; ch 5, shell in next ch-3 lp; ch 3, sk next ch-3 lp, (sc in next ch-3 lp, ch 3) 3 times; shell in next shell; dc in next dc, (ch 1, dc in next dc) twice; rep from * across to last dc; dc in last dc, ch 1, dc in 3rd ch of turning ch-4; ch 4, turn.

Row 7: Dc in next dc; * shell in next shell; ch 3, sk next ch-3 lp, (sc in next ch-3 lp, ch 3) twice; shell in next shell; ch 5, shell in next ch-5 lp; ch 5, shell in next shell; ch 3, sk next ch-3 lp, (sc in next ch-3 lp, ch 3) twice; sk next ch-3 lp, shell in next shell; dc in next dc, (ch 1, dc in next dc) twice; rep from * across to last dc; dc in last dc, ch 1, dc in 3rd ch of turning ch-4; ch 4, turn.

Row 8: Dc in next dc; * shell in next shell; ch 3, sk next ch-3 lp, sc in next ch-3 lp, ch 3, shell in next shell; ch 3, 5 dc in next ch-5 lp; ch 3, shell in next shell; ch 3, 5 dc in next ch-5 lp; ch 3, shell in next shell; ch 3, sk next ch-3 lp, sc in next ch-3 lp, ch 3, shell in next shell; dc in next dc, (ch 1, dc in next dc) twice; rep from * across to last dc; dc in last dc, ch 1, dc in 3rd ch of turning ch-4; ch 4, turn.

Row 9: Dc in next dc; * shell in each of next 2 shells; † (ch 1, dc in next dc) 5 times; ch 1, shell in next shell †; rep from † to † once more; shell in next shell; dc in next dc, (ch 1, dc in next dc) twice; rep from * across to last dc; dc in last dc, ch 1, dc in 3rd ch of turning ch-4; ch 4, turn.

Row 10: Dc in next dc; * CL in top of first CL of next shell; shell in next shell; † ch 1, dc in next dc, (ch 2, dc in next dc) 4 times; ch 1, shell in next shell †; rep from † to † once more; CL in 2nd CL of next shell; dc in next dc, (ch 1, dc in next dc) twice; rep from * across to last dc; dc in last dc, ch 1, dc in 3rd ch of turning ch-4; ch 4, turn.

Rep Rows 5 through 10 for pattern.

18 + 4 chs

#101

Multiple of 18 + 4

> **PATTERN STITCH**
>
> **Popcorn** (PC): 3 dc in next lp, drop lp from hook, insert hook in first dc, draw dropped lp through, ch 1: PC made.

Row 1: Dc in 4th ch from hook; * sk next 2 chs, in next ch work (dc, ch 1, dc); rep from * across to last 3 chs; sk next 2 chs, 2 dc in last ch; ch 3, turn.

Row 2 (right side): Dc in first dc, in next ch-1 sp work (dc, ch 1, dc); * ch 5, sk next ch-1 sp, sc in next ch-1 sp, ch 5, sk next ch-1 sp, in each of next 3 ch-1 sps work (dc, ch 1, dc); rep from * across to beg 3 skipped chs; 2 dc in 3rd ch of 3 skipped chs; ch 3, turn.

Row 3: Dc in first dc, in next ch-1 sp work (dc, ch 1, dc); * (ch 3, sc in next ch-5 lp) twice; ch 3, in each of next 3 ch-1 sps work (dc, ch 1, dc); rep from * across to turning ch; 2 dc in 3rd ch of turning ch-3; ch 3, turn.

Row 4: Dc in first dc, in next ch-1 sp work (dc, ch 1, dc); * sk next ch-3 lp, in next ch-3 lp work [PC (see Pattern Stitch), ch 3, PC, ch 3, PC]; sk next ch-3 lp, in each of next 3 ch-1 sps work (dc, ch 1, dc); rep from * across to turning ch; 2 dc in 3rd ch of turning ch-3; ch 3, turn.

Row 5: Dc in first dc, in next ch-1 sp work (dc, ch 1, dc); * (ch 3, sc in next ch-3 lp) twice; ch 3, in each of next 3 ch-1 sps work (dc, ch 1, dc); rep from * across to turning ch; 2 dc in 3rd ch of turning ch-3; ch 3, turn.

Row 6: Dc in first dc, in next ch-1 sp work (dc, ch 1, dc); * in each of next 3 ch-3 lps work (dc, ch 1, dc); in each of next 3 ch-1 sps work (dc, ch 1, dc); rep from * across to turning ch; 2 dc in 3rd ch of turning ch-3; ch 3, turn.

Row 7: Dc in first dc, in next ch-1 sp work (dc, ch 1, dc); * ch 5, sk next ch-1 sp, sc in next ch-1 sp, ch 5, sk next ch-1 sp, in each of next 3 ch-1 sps work (dc, ch 1, dc); rep from * across to turning ch; 2 dc in 3rd ch of turning ch-3; ch 3, turn.

Rep Rows 3 through 7 for pattern.